SUSAN SAY

God's People
at Worship
Together

Accessible worship for the
whole church community

COMMON WORSHIP RESOURCE

**kevin
mayhew**

First published in 2003 by

KEVIN MAYHEW LTD
Buxhall, Stowmarket, Suffolk, IP14 3BW
E-mail: info@kevinmayhewltd.com

KINGSGATE PUBLISHING INC
1000 Pannell Street, Suite G, Columbia, MO 65201
E-mail: sales@kingsgatepublishing.com

9 8 7 6 5 4 3 2 1 0

ISBN 1 84417 187 6
Catalogue No 1500673

Cover design by Angela Selfe
Edited by Katherine Laidler
Typesetting by Louise Selfe

Printed in Great Britain

Contents

Foreword

This book is primarily a resource for when the whole church community meets together. Often known as 'all-age worship', such occasions still fill many of us with dread because they are so hard to do. It is really difficult to hold together the varied needs, likes and dislikes of such a diverse congregation, and there are bound to be conflicts as everyone struggles to come to terms with the 'family' requirement of give and take, share and compromise which all-age worship entails. How much easier it would be to worship in our separate age groups and avoid all those problems. How much easier to justify our fragmentation rather than facing up to what it says about our identity as God's 'People'.

There is no easy solution to the problems; it's true that worshipping with all ages present is never an easy option. It is fraught with difficulties of balance and inclusion, often viewed suspiciously by those of all the age groups, and an enterprise which is bound to be demanding in terms of communication, tolerance, patience, mutual respect and consideration.

Yet what are these qualities if not the very stones of which a loving community is built? They tackle self-centredness in the challenging practice of loving service, and provide the very opportunities we need to learn what it means to be members of one Body in Christ.

Rather than taking the widespread and easier option of splitting the church community into strata so as to avoid the hassle of being 'one', we can view those challenges as possibilities for learning the lessons of sharing and responsible belonging. When as a church we make the commitment to worship all together on some occasions, we are affirming the fundamental truth that, however counter-cultural it feels, to work at becoming God's People as a community is an important and essential sign of the kingdom.

In this book we explore what it means to be God's People and how that might be best expressed in our worship. We then work this out in practical suggestions for each season of the Church's year, and each Sunday of the three-year lectionary.

The challenge

Community or 'plural individualism'?

What's the difference between a group of people sharing a coach on a commuter train and a group of people celebrating a family wedding? We might see the first as separate individuals who happen to be travelling together for the moment, whereas the second is a deliberately gathered community, with individuals drawn to share an event that is important to them all. Simply being there and being part of one another is an essential aspect of the celebration. The people at the wedding haven't stopped being individuals, but this gathering focuses on what they share. The very word 'comm-unity' means something like 'coming together as one'.

There's quite a lot spoken about community in our culture at the moment. We often hear people voicing their concern that 'community seems to have broken down' and 'where's the community spirit disappeared to?' Others talk about strategies to 'build or re-build community' in areas of social deprivation, and we have plenty of 'community centres' and 'community health councils'. At the same time we are conscious of the shift that has taken place in our lives concerning the focus of community. Since we all move around far more, and extended families are rarely settled in one locality, we know that the old idea of community based on geographical location and traditional extended family sits uncomfortably with the reality. That doesn't mean it's wrong – it's just different.

What's interesting is that people obviously like the idea of community very much, and establish it wherever they are. Lunch-hour pubs, the covered entrance to a back door where the smokers congregate, sports, hobbies and shared politics or faith – we all form communities based on our choices. Generally this system seems to satisfy our need and wish to feel part of a community, but we also need to recognise that there is a sense in which it alters our perception of what community is. Driven strongly by personal choice, it looks more and more like 'plural individualism' rather than 'inter-related unity', which assumes mutual commitment and support regardless of shared interest or age group. You can choose your friends, but you don't get to choose extended family or (to some extent) neighbours.

Perhaps that's one of the reasons for our fascination with the *Big Brother* type of reality programme: people lumped together having to live 'in community' has become an endangered and rare species which we like to cage and observe. As spectators we are enthralled by the ingenious ways people wrestle with the difficulties of being members of a community.

Within our own households, of course, we know all too well the joys and problems of living together under one roof,

Tell the whole congregation of Israel that on the tenth of this month they are to take a lamb for each family, a lamb for each household.
Exodus 12:3

When in the future your child asks you, 'What does this mean?' you shall answer . . . *Exodus 13:14*

Make them known to your children and your children's children.
Deuteronomy 4:9

Assemble the people for me, and I will let them hear my words, so that they may learn to fear me as long as they live on the earth, and may teach their children to do so.
Deuteronomy 4:10

Now the boy Samuel did not yet know the Lord . . . And the Lord called again, 'Samuel! Samuel!' . . .
1 Samuel 3

'There is still the youngest,' Jesse answered, 'but he is keeping the sheep.' And Samuel said to Jesse, 'Send and bring him; for we will not sit down until he comes here.'
1 Samuel 16:11

Saul said to David, '. . . You are just a boy . . .' But David said to Saul, 'The Lord, who saved me from the paw of the lion and from the paw of the bear, will save me from the hand of this Philistine.' So Saul said to David, 'Go, and may the Lord be with you!'
1 Samuel 17

. . . and all the people rejoiced . . .
2 Chronicles 29:36

The priests were enrolled with all their little children, their wives, their sons, and their daughters, the whole multitude; for they were faithful in keeping themselves holy.
2 Chronicles 31:18

In the eighth year of his reign, while he was still a boy, he began to seek the God of his ancestor David.
2 Chronicles 34:3

The king went up to the house of the Lord with all the people both great and small; he read in their hearing all the words of the book of the covenant . . . *2 Chronicles 34:30*

And all the people responded with a great shout when they praised the Lord. *Ezra 3:11*

All the people sat in the open square before the house of God, trembling because of this matter and because of the heavy rain. *Ezra 10:9*

To these four young men God gave knowledge and skill . . . *Daniel 1:17*

Then afterwards I will pour out my spirit on all flesh; your sons and your daughters shall prophesy, your old men shall dream dreams, and your young men shall see visions. Even on the male and female slaves, in those days, I will pour out my spirit. *Joel 2:28-29*

All the people gathered together in the square before the Water Gate . . . The priest Ezra brought the law before the assembly, both men and women and all who could hear with understanding . . . Also the Levites helped the people to understand the law . . . They gave the sense so that the people understood the reading. *Nehemiah 8:16*

Out of the mouths of infants and children you have ordained praise. *Psalm 8:2*

Young men and maidens, old men and children, let them praise the name of the Lord. *Psalm 148*

and we all spend our money on avoiding the difficulties as much as we can, using wealth to enable the 'plural individualism' model and banish the bother of the more challenging kind of community living. Just think how normal it is to buy larger and more separate housing units if we happen to get richer. We enjoy buying individual space. We buy separation from neighbours. The more televisions per household, the less we need to share and compromise over which channel to watch. We seem to be working hard at leaving community skills behind us, so that we now need special training in areas like conflict management, citizenship, child safety and parenting.

All this is so much a natural part of our culture that we take the fracturing for granted. We accept the huge barriers that have built up between the young and the older, and even rush around with extra cement to strengthen those solid walls. We pick up on the marketplace values of rigidly defined styles, and apply them as if they are the whole story, rather than a business enterprise. 'Family holiday' is likely to mean spending the barest minimum of time together as a family, with all the different age groups 'catered for' with a full programme of their own. Of course, everyone can have a wonderful time on such a holiday, and I'm glad they do, but what does it say about our understanding of community? I wonder if we have tried so hard to sanitise it, and sand down the rough places in it, that we are in danger of losing it altogether? And that makes me wonder if the Church is actually called to be prophetic here – somewhat counter-cultural in the area of community?

Being a sign of the kingdom of God

It is perhaps significant that the current theological focus on the Trinity coincides with the widely discerned breakdown of 'community spirit' in our culture, fragmented through long emphasis on individualism. The darker effects of individualism seem thankfully to have alerted us to recognise in the concept of the Trinity the social nature of God, in whose likeness we have been made, and hence our community identity as persons. In typical human style we only realise the beauty and significance of community when it has already seriously eroded.

Like a vehicle screeching to a desperate halt at the edge of a cliff, we humans tend to respond well to such threatening disasters in crisis mode, once it dawns on us that the disaster is imminent. Words like 'co-operative' and 'collaborative' suddenly spring up everywhere to realign our thinking, and step by hesitant step we set ourselves to learn again those lessons of loving one another within the love of God. In the process we discover that there are enormous benefits to those within the faith community, and in the context of our society and our world. The challenges become opportunities for grace, and the spiritual Body of the western Church, grown flabby and complacent by the fragmentation made possible through our wealth, finds itself flexing stiffened muscles and creaking joints. There is a freshness and flexibility which comes of knowing, loving and valuing one another across the whole age and culture range, which we have almost forgotten, and must set ourselves to rediscover.

What Jesus was announcing and preparing, after all, built on the rock of human forgiven sinners like Peter, was a new kind of kingdom, which was to take the form of a community – a People. He had already gathered about him an exceedingly diverse group of individuals, and they were bound together through their common calling by Jesus, rather than personal choice to be with one another. In fact, the Gospel accounts hint often at the tensions and irritations, competing and attention-seeking that went on among the disciples. Clearly Jesus hadn't chosen them for mutual compatibility, any more than the *Big Brother* producers do. Rather, part of the disciples' training as rock-members of the young Church is to learn to live together in forgiving love, and they get plenty of practice. They don't find it any easier than the rest of us!

All the same, that community of loving is their calling, and the term 'church' reflects this, with its root 'ecclesia' meaning 'called out from'. So if we, too, are to be true to our calling, perhaps we need to take a candid look at the current understanding of community in our culture and check that as church we are not confusing the widespread 'pluralised individualism' with the vigorous, challenging model of community Jesus envisages as being for the world a sign of the kingdom of God.

So what can we pick up from the teaching of Jesus about community living? Fundamental is what Jesus proclaims to sum up the whole of the Law and the prophets:

> Jesus replied, 'Love the Lord your God with all your heart and with all your soul and with all your mind. This is the first and greatest commandment. And the second is like it: Love your neighbour as yourself.' All the Law and the Prophets hang on these two commandments.
>
> *Matthew 22:37-40*

Many of the parables explore what this loving entails, and it becomes clear that the expectation is of enormous generosity towards one another, putting ourselves out for one another, getting involved with the practical and often unattractive caring and sharing, an extravagance in forgiveness from which it is natural to flinch, a respect which crosses all boundaries and refuses to have any truck with oppression or pomposity, and a humility which counts all opportunity for menial service a great privilege.

We find Jesus telling stories about practical help expected to take precedence over liturgical ruling, about debts being wiped out only when the indebted starts cancelling debts owed to him, and about Godly generosity not being linked

. . . the disciples came to Jesus and asked, 'Who is the greatest in the kingdom of heaven?' He called a child, whom he put among them, and said, 'Truly I tell you, unless you change and become like children, you will never enter the kingdom of heaven. Whoever becomes humble like this child is the greatest in the kingdom of heaven. Whoever welcomes one such child in my name welcomes me.' *Matthew 18:1-5*

'Whoever wants to be first must be last of all and servant of all.' Then he took a little child and put it among them; and taking it in his arms, he said to them, 'Whoever welcomes one such child in my name, welcomes me, and whoever welcomes me welcomes not me but the one who sent me.' *Mark 9:35-37*

Then he ordered them to get all the people to sit down in groups on the green grass. So they sat down in groups of hundreds and of fifties . . . And all ate and were filled; and they took up twelve baskets full of broken pieces and of the fish. *Mark 6:39-42*

People were bringing even infants to him that he might touch them; and when the disciples saw it, they sternly ordered them not to do it. But Jesus called for them and said, 'Let the children come to me, and do not stop them; for it is to such as these that the kingdom of God belongs. *Luke 18:15-16*

Truly I tell you, whoever does not receive the kingdom of God as a little child will never enter it. *Luke 18:17*

But when the chief priests and scribes . . . heard the children crying out in the temple, 'Hosanna to the Son of David', they became angry and said to him, 'Do you hear what these children are saying?' Jesus said to them, 'Yes; have you never read, "Out of the mouths of infants and nursing babies you have prepared praise for yourself"?' *Matthew 21:15-16*

'All these I have kept since I was a boy.' *Mark 10:20*

'I thank you, Father, Lord of heaven and earth, because you have hidden these things from the wise and intelligent and have revealed them to infants . . .' *Luke 10:21*

'Is there anyone among you who, if your child asks for a fish, will give a snake instead of a fish?' *Luke 11:11*

Some of the Pharisees in the crowd said to him, 'Teacher, order your disciples to stop.' He answered, 'I tell you, if these were silent, the stones would shout out.' *Luke 19:39-40*

'There is a boy here who has two barley loaves and two fish. But what are they among so many?' Jesus said, 'Make the people sit down.' *John 6:9-10*

Now the whole group of those who believed were of one heart and soul, and no one claimed private ownership of any possessions, but everything they owned was held in common. *Acts 4:32*

Peter went to the house of Mary, the mother of John whose other name was Mark, where many had gathered and were praying. When he knocked at the outer gate a maid named Rhoda came to answer. *Acts 12:12*

And the witnesses laid their coats at the feet of a young man named Saul. While they were stoning Stephen . . . he shouted out in a loud voice, 'Lord, do not hold this sin against them.' *Acts 7:59-60*

to hours of service put in. We find accepted values and hierarchies stood on their head, and a little child used as the example of how to receive the kingdom of heaven. Even enemies are not to be hated 'with a perfect hatred'* but loved.

All this is loving with a rugged toughness, rather than the gentle, fluffy sort we tend to prefer. But as Jesus pointed out, if we only love those who love us, how are we to be a sign of God's kingdom, since that is normal human behaviour and requires no rigorous generosity or self denial at all? Somehow we manage to hear the words of the gospel and squash them into the shape and colour which suits us, rather than hearing them and adapting our own mind and heart-set to fit what's really there. We might smile indulgently at the Victorian idea of helping only 'the deserving poor' but few of us actually sustain friendships with those we find difficult, whether individually or internationally, or continue to work at relationships in church which rub. We're far more likely to avoid eye contact which might invite conversation, and few of us are prepared to 'get involved' with anyone we suspect may turn into a long-term drain on our friendship resources.

Of course, there are good reasons for our reticence. We are to include ourselves in those we love and care for, and it is sensible to sit down and count costs before committing ourselves to tower-building. But I still think we have become artists at toning down the colour of the gospel to a muted call we can comfortably fit into our existing life style, rather than recognising the drastic change to outlook and mindset which the Jesus kingdom suggests.

In retrospect, at least, the Church honours and values those who stick out their necks and engage with the gospel colour in such a full-bodied way that gospel shockwaves shake the communities in which they live. Think of Francis and his companions, joyfully abandoning wealth and embracing poverty. Think of Jackie Pullinger befriending the heroine users, Corrie ten Boom with her working knowledge of deepest forgiveness, Lord Shaftesbury and Doctor Barnardo responding with practical help to those in desperate need, or Mother Teresa lavishing love with respect on the destitute and dying she found on the streets. In different ways all of these saintly people have been considered fools for taking the gospel to heart in such a practical way, yet they stand tall and authentic with the light of Christ shining in their lives. It is not those who cry 'Lord! Lord!' who enter the kingdom, but those who 'do' the will of the Father.

When I was preparing to talk at one training day on all-age worship I thought it might be an idea to look at some scripture references to the whole people of God gathering to worship. I have to say I was quite shocked to find how many such references there were, as we often brush past them without noticing. So in case you are interested, or need persuading that there is good, sound biblical evidence that God calls us

---

* Psalm 139:22, *Authorised Version.*

as a People, these words of scripture are here on either side of you as you read, and I hope that all our thinking and planning of worship may always keep them in view.

The call to follow Christ is a call to a great adventure, an adventure we undertake as a community, even when for most of the week we live dispersed, carrying our community identity within us. Regular gathering of this complete-age-range community of Christ-followers is an essential part of our identity and our calling. We learn the way of love by walking along it. The inevitable rubs and conflicts of worshipping regularly together are actually beautiful in their potential for training us as the love community we are called to be. I'm going to say that again in case you missed it: they are actually beautiful. And our instinctive avoidance of the training ground offered is itself a symptom we need to address with humility.

I am reminded of your sincere faith, a faith that lived first in your grandmother Lois and your mother Eunice and now, I am sure, lives in you. *2 Timothy 1:5*

How can we 'do' worshipping together?

Well, perhaps I have convinced you that worshipping together regularly as a full community is important and worthwhile in spite of the difficulties. But how is this to be done?

Although in this book I am focusing on the worship, we can't look at this in isolation. To worship together as a community will partly entail living together as a community, and that may well be like a young plant you have just collected from the garden centre. It will need the right conditions to grow, and it will need looking after.

If there are never any events that involve all ages together, people won't get to know who they are. If there is never a communal task undertaken for the good of those beyond the church walls, people will never get to learn that church is supposed to be turned outwards, rather than inwards, since it doesn't exist for its own upkeep.

So one of the most important ways in which we can begin to 'do' worshipping together is to look at what is already happening involving all ages, checking that it becomes a regular way of life. Parties, picnics, fairs, dances, pantomimes, holidays or pilgrimages all come into this category. Even recognising that they've been happening for years already can help us thank God for them rather than take such community for granted. And check what generous-hearted community projects you are or could be involved in as a church. Things like carol singing, supportive link-ups with a church in another part of the world, sponsored events, hosting exchanges, drop-in cafés, or dads and children clubs. The actual events will vary according to location and need, of course, but healthy churches are not just self-supporting – they have this foolish urge to give away rather than store up, which somehow makes them rich.

It's in this wider context that we can talk about worship. I want to suggest first some general principles which can help in all our thinking and planning, whatever the season or the particular readings provided. You may find they also lay to rest some fears and concerns you might have, and if you take these basic principles on board, the planning and leading of all-age worship will be far less of a burden and far more fun.

Some general principles

The whole community

All-age worship is about people of all ages being enabled to meet with God as part of the community of Christ-followers. So it is not children's worship, or young people's worship, or worship for the middle-aged, but worship for God's People. This is God's Community Touching Base.

Not a performance

All-age worship is not about entertainment or performance. It is the work of the People of God, and everyone present is involved in this duty and joy.

Accessibility

All-age worship is about accessibility. Worship that is too wordy will not be accessible to everyone. Words can create barriers between cultures and age groups, and leave out those who don't understand. Use the senses as well as the words, the emotions as well as the intellect, the shared experiences of being human.

Unity, not uniformity

All-age worship doesn't mean that everyone has to be doing the same thing all the time. At the deepest level they are, of course, but responding to the word of God, praying and worshipping can vary according to personality as much as age group, and provision can be made for this.

Flexibility and imagination

There are no rules stating that we all have to sit still for worship, standing from time to time to sing from a book. Smaller congregations have the advantage of being able to move around the church building as part of the liturgy, for instance, and many find this – often to their surprise – most helpful and conducive to prayer.

Differentiation

Nothing needs to be rejected for fear of some present being unable to understand. In times of praise and worship God can touch people's hearts in many different ways, by no means all of them involving intellectual understanding. And who can claim to understand the mysteries of God anyway?

Humility

When we gather to worship we are not to lord it over one another in any way but walk humbly with our God, not controlling but open to his leading; not manipulative but enabling; listening properly to one another, even when there is disagreement, and learning from one another, even when it means losing face. It isn't our mistakes that grieve God's heart, but our insistence that there haven't been any.

Regular review

You may find these general principles helpful as a guideline in your planning of worship, and in the ongoing assessment and review. At least once a year take time to go away somewhere beautiful and quiet, to pray together in silence, attentive to God and without any great plans, simply working to be as open and available as possible. Any thoughts that come to mind as part of this shared experience should be discussed in the context of worship, so that everyone is constantly reminded of this being God's business in which we are called to share. There are far too many takeover bids that jeopardise the growth of the kingdom. Let God lead the community into worship which feeds, inspires and touches earth with heaven.

So let's get practical

Having in mind the principles described above, we can now take a walk around the different areas of worship, and see how we can make them as accessible to all ages and personalities as possible.

Holy space

Let's take a fresh look at these buildings we know as 'churches'. To some extent the architecture of our buildings defines our use of them in worship, and, of course, each church building reflects not current thinking and culture but that of the age in which it was built.

So we find, for instance, that many traditional churches were built long and narrow, with everyone apart from the choir facing east, and the altar or holy table against the far east wall. Priest and people all gazed in the same direction as they worshipped.

Many were originally designed without the pews, and certainly the rigidity of pews cuts down on flexibility. If your church is in a position to replace pews with more versatile seating arrangements, you will find the whole building opened up with all kinds of possibilities for worship, so that is seriously worth considering. If, on the other hand, your pews are a beautiful and integral part of the building, there are still advantages and ways to use them effectively.

Many church buildings have been steeped in prayer for generations and are places of space and peace which many still value, whether they are regular churchgoers or not. The simplest and least formalised possibility of all-age worship is to have set times when the church is open for people to wander around, either in silence or with music playing or singing going on. Think of your flower festival in this way and imagine the possibilities. Around the church there could be different focuses for prayer and thanksgiving, penitence and reflection. Design a number of trails around the church, like nature trails but guiding people around the stained glass windows with short meditations provided, for instance. Or lead them around the Christian faith, moving from door to font, to lectern, to cross, to altar. Use the Stations of the Cross, or the banners, or a candle stand. Have simple activities available around the church – colouring in a short text, dipping hands in water, tracing over stonework with a finger, and so on.

Through the building allow people of all ages the opportunity to touch the faith of generations and experience God's loving presence in this holy place, without feeling they have to take part in the organised worship which many fear.

During more formal times of worship, too, there are many opportunities to use our church buildings far more. The times set aside for confession, intercession, sermon or communion can all be used sometimes in this way, with the building doing the speaking and drawing people into God's presence.

Finally, the preparation of the building for worship and the maintenance of its nature as a place of prayer need also to be the responsibility and joy of the whole community. Imagine a church building where day by day cleaners, flower arrangers and pray-ers of all ages regularly come in. The main reason church buildings are closed is that the people are not praying there. The habit has got lost. But we can reverse that and turn our churches into the welcoming, open resources of peace they were built to be. The world is not asking us to put on more services but simply to be more available. We need to listen to that request.

Services

Specific times of worship – services, as we call them – have hidden in their title the understanding of gathering for worship being in itself an act of serving. The picture is of us all being 'staff' or 'servants below stairs', preparing, looking after needs, providing, offering, all in a climate of honour and respect, both of God and one another. I don't think it's such a bad picture, really. Certainly a lot better than the idea of a few professionals doing things up front while most of us sit as onlookers or audience. A great deal better than the idea that we are only coming to worship for what we get out of it, and, by implication, if the menu isn't to our taste, we don't need to be there.

The whole point of gathered worship is that God has invited us. We are both servants and guests. All of us are invited guests of God, and that includes the ones up front as well. You're not being invited by the vicar, or the church-wardens, or the church, but by God. And all of us present, whatever our status in society, our height or shoe-size, are workers in this business of serving. It's an attitude of mind that affects what goes on. We are all there to engage with God, to be attentive to God, to learn the loving he made us for. And being together provides us with a perfect way to do this with our feet firmly on the ground.

Welcoming people and being genuinely interested in them is worship. Dressing up carefully in clean, ironed robes and holding a candle, presiding at the Eucharist, or singing in a choir reverently and as well as you can, is worship. Noticing when someone can't find the place and helping them, or using your own book, even if you know the words off by heart, is worship. By your own Godliness, drawing others to seek him, is worship. Dancing happily to the hymns with a streamer or a stick of bells, and enjoying the coloured light from the windows or the rays of sunlight glinting on polished wood, is worship. Drawing your best picture, preaching your best sermon, pulling your wandering thoughts back firmly whenever they wander, all this is worship. Coming to a service which is not your favourite, so as to welcome others and pray for them throughout, is worship.

I suppose it's all tied up with that idea of Psalm 50: 'Whoever offers me a sacrifice of thanksgiving honours me.' And then, of course, Jesus returns the compliment, washing our feet, feeding and restoring us to wholeness, and beautifully teaching us about real service by his humility and loving care of us all.

Music

Music has long been linked closely with worship. Somehow it has the power to resonate with the spiritual in us, touching the heart and evoking deep emotions. Film producers use it to create a particular atmosphere and render the images more effective. Advertisers use it to coax us into a particular frame of mind where we are more likely to hear their message. Dentists sometimes use it to calm their patients. And while we may not agree about the style, we love taking music with us everywhere, from the shower to our cars when we travel. Particular pieces of music are frequently requested for weddings and for funerals.

Clearly music is a wonderful resource to use, and church buildings are often lofty places where the sound gets lifted up and celebrated by the space. It is worth getting equipment to make the most of the acoustics, as recorded sounds and music can be so valuable in worship, and a library of CDs (or a list of who to borrow from) is very helpful.

Recorded music

Use recorded sounds and music

- as scene-setters before and during a scripture reading
- as an aid to reflection following a reading or talk
- as background during times of penitence or intercession
- and as a quietening, calming invitation to worship while people are coming into church.

Film soundtracks are particularly useful, since they are designed to be unobtrusive and work well as background music. Try some pieces for single instruments, such as flute, or cello, panpipes or drum. Try world music samplers. Some of the music collections of calming, romantic or uplifting music are also good, as are the natural sounds of lapping water, ocean surf, mountain streams, rainstorms, wind and birdsong.

Using the organ

Many churches have organ music as the norm. Organ music is wonderfully versatile, with the possibility of faint, gentle and distant sounds right through to the air-shaking thundering of full voice. Rather than being used only as an accompaniment to hymns, organ music can also lead people into quietness before a service, sing out their praise as they stand silently adoring, or draw people down into silence from glorious, rich exuberance. Music is available now to help organists broaden their repertoire to include this kind of central leading of worship rather than being used merely as an accompanist. Rediscovering the organ as a worship resource is, I feel, far preferable to abandoning such a creative instrument. And for those who have no organist, but love the sound of organ music sometimes in their worship, there are CDs available which can work well.

Music groups A music group leading worship is in some ways a return to the days before the organ's popularity. There is something about a group of players and the varied instruments that speaks about the very community calling we are concerned to foster. At its best such a group is acting out the give and take, the harmony and resolved tensions of a loving community, and being able to see the group members seems to encourage people to sing. In such cases the music group is genuinely leading people to worship, rather than performing to an audience.

There can be different styles of music groups, of course, and they don't have to include drums and guitars. In some churches a classical music sound would be more appropriate, or a steel band, recorder consort or jazz. It's a question of taking off the 's'posed to be' blinkers and looking at what instruments people actually play and/or would like to play. All age groups can play in a band if it includes open string and two-note parts, simple percussion and bells. (Small bells are really useful because however enthusiastically they're shaken, they never become obtrusive.)

Choirs Choirs are another all-age resource which gets ignored sometimes. The lovely combination of young and adult voices has always been prized, and the Royal College of Church Music will gladly provide guidance and support the training of singers. Local arts councils can offer grants for providing such a choir in a neighbourhood, particularly in urban priority areas.

For some odd reason there is a suspicion that when all ages are present all excellence has to be discarded, yet I can think of nothing further from the truth. A well-trained church choir of children, young people and adults can be a marvellous example of and opportunity for all-age worship, developing all those loving community skills of listening, respecting one another, self-control, and working together singing different melodies but in harmony. And that's a good lesson to learn.

Even if you don't have a regular choir, it's still an idea to invite those who enjoy singing (all age groups, of course) to sing their worship from time to time while other people worship in different ways, such as walking around the building, drawing or praying quietly.

Another possibility is to invite singers of all ages in the area to take part in a monthly candlelit choral evensong from scratch, perhaps on a Saturday late afternoon. Singers come for a practice just before the service, and worship using the beautiful and time-honoured traditional service for the evening. Not only can such a project become a significant part of a local arts programme, but it is also an act of mission, reaching out to those who might never otherwise engage in public worship.

What is vital is that choir members are always made aware that they are there to worship and encourage others to worship. At Taizé in France, all practice times are considered part of the worship, and this transforms the music. It is as important to work on the spiritual nurture of a choir as its musical skill, and the responsibility for such prayerful leadership cannot be carried by the choir leader alone. Every choir needs a spiritual director as well, so that practices begin and end with prayer, and an expectation of worship during services is encouraged and helped to develop.

It must be recognised that very often tensions and conflicts can arise between music directors and church leaders. Both need the committed prayer support of the whole church, together with God's abundant grace, to help them work through difficulties with integrity and generosity of spirit. Hard as this may be, the kingdom grows through such conflicts faithfully and forgivingly addressed.

Hymns and songs

Yet another myth is that if children are going to be part of the worship, only simple songs and hymns can be sung. Any of the traditionally well-loved classics will not do because young children can't understand or read the language. But, of course, the reason such hymns become so well known and loved is that they were once sung by people as children, and the words, perhaps barely understood at first, have stayed in the memory, becoming a source of strength and inspiration when in adulthood the words suddenly make life-giving sense.

We cheat our children of spiritual treasure when we downsize everything in this way. We don't do it with food, or household furniture or travel. Instead we adapt to enable the children to take part in these adult things, with child seats in the car, a step to reach the wash-basin, and small portions at restaurants. Children are notorious for wanting to do the grown-up thing anyway, and there is a great danger that if children feel condescension in worship, they won't want to be involved. Neither will it be possible to cater for those too old for the childish but too young to feel like indulging the children. There are many excellent hymns and songs suitable for both children and adults, but the classics also need to be given a place during worship of the whole gathered community. So how do we cater for all age groups, where hymns and songs are concerned?

Hymns and songs consist of voiced words, written words, and music. That gives us plenty of opportunity for responding and worshipping in different ways and at different levels as we worship together.

For instance:

- While one of the traditional classic hymns is being sung by those who can read the words and sing the melody, non-readers and whole-body worshippers can express their worship through dancing or using streamers or flags, responding to the call and sense of the melody. (This is not about performance, so they do not even need to be near the front – just in a space. The streamers can be given out from a special basket labelled 'For Worship', to make the point.)

- Teach some of the children to sign or action one of the classic, traditional hymns. The act of signing helps their own understanding as well as providing a valuable service for others. And whether or not they are actually singing, the hymn is becoming familiar to them.
- Sometimes a chorus is easy to learn by heart, and this can be what everyone sings together, with young children playing bells or quiet shakers through the verses.
- Sometimes have a verse for women and girls to sing together, or men and boys. Non-readers singing to 'la' is fine.

Scripture reading

Such an integral part of worship is often prepared with a surprisingly casual approach. The public reading of scripture in our churches can be one of the most powerful influences on people's lives and their faith journey, yet so often the passages are barely glanced at before a reading, which makes the lack of understanding of the text very clear indeed. There is such arrogance in this, isn't there? How dare we be so slovenly in our calling to proclaim the gospel? How often have words of life been missed or misunderstood, and lives left unchanged because of our careless approach to reading the scriptures publicly?

One of the most obvious ways to make worship accessible, whatever the tradition of the church, is to address our generally appalling Bible-reading skills and present people of all ages with the words of life proclaimed in such a way that they are freed to speak right into hearts and lives. Never mind all the other exciting and imaginative ways we can bring the Bible to life for people – let's start with learning to read!

Training

Train everyone who reads the Bible in worship. If there is no one with such training skills in your church, get in touch with the local school or theatre and ask for some help. This is an urgent matter.

Advance booking

Make sure readers know what they are expected to read well in advance, and write on their rota suggestions for good preparation. This is not simply checking out pronunciation and sentence structure but meaning as well. It might be sensible to set up a helpline to deal with any queries, and check that preparation is happening. It doesn't take much to sharpen up everyone's sense of responsibility, especially if at the top of each rota is a sentence explaining the importance of this ministry.

Feedback

Give all readers practice with the sound system in a group session which creates an expectation of an important job worth doing well. Such communal training and feedback helps build a supportive and rigorous approach.

Rehydration

Printed words are like dehydrated thoughts – much like lentils or cup-a-soups. If we read them neat, the listener has to work hard at rehydrating them into thoughts before they mean very much. A good reader rehydrates those marks on the paper by *thinking and imagining the scene as they read*, so that what the listeners hear is not words but the very thoughts, and a passage can suddenly spring to life in this way.

Real, not affected

Fancy, dramatic renderings just get in the way of the meaning.

Using the senses

Our human life is an orchestration of mind, heart, senses, emotions, memories and dreams, and a whole lot more. Worship reaches deep into our human 'being' when we are encouraged to engage with God on all these levels. The visual, tactile and aural not only help us to understand but attune us spiritually to respond with heart as well as mind. Let's go through the main sections of a service and see how the senses can be used effectively.

As we gather for worship

What people see and hear as they come into church will affect their attitude and how they feel. Think about the kind of atmosphere you want to create and then use sound and image and action to help it happen. If, for instance, you want people of all ages to sense the awe and wonder of God in the beauty of holiness, choose music with a sense of 'otherness' and mystery, have the preparations done early so that the worship leaders are visibly in place praying, use candlelight and flowers, project an image of God's good creation, and clear the clutter, so there is a sense of spaciousness. Clean the windows. Polish furniture and metal so everything gleams. Don't expect everyone to catch on to your atmosphere at first, but persist in these quiet signals of peace and eventually, whether in a few minutes or a few months, you'll find people being drawn into the quality of stillness and reverence.

Times of penitence, confession and assurance of God's forgiveness

To give people space for gathering their thoughts and feelings, play music which picks up on the ache of longing. Celtic, Middle Eastern and Asian melodies often seem particularly good at this. Or use sounds, like the sea or whales singing or wolves. Or try a sense of the ancient as we get in touch with the vulnerability and the hope of our human nature. Give people something to touch and hold as they think and reflect, simple and linked with the focus of the day. Sometimes make a walked journey from seat to cross or seat to font a tangible part of the penitence and forgiveness. Use projected images to nudge us into recognising our part in allowing injustice and oppression to flourish unopposed. Let people come physically to the foot of the cross and lay down a symbol of their penitence and desire for God's healing forgiveness.

The Gloria

Project images of the glory of creation with the first sentence of the Gloria superimposed on them. Or have huge sheets of lining paper, big brushes or sponges, protect the area and invite a few people to paint their praise big and bright and colourful as everyone sings out God's praise.

The readings

Project images appropriate to the challenge or atmosphere of a particular reading. Use mime while a narrative passage is being read. Make costumes, which can be used throughout the year on occasions, rather than simply at Christmas. Use sounds and music to create the atmosphere and for reflection following the reading. Involve people in the script, both as individuals and as a group, with the words either printed out, projected or written on speech-bubble shapes.

The talk/sermon/homily

Check that the loop system works effectively. Have someone signing if necessary. Use the OHP to draw the message as it's being preached, or use it as a light box with silhouettes to illustrate. Make paper and pencils available for right-brained people of all ages, for attentive doodling, which can be displayed after the service as a basis for further discussion. Use three-dimensional metaphors, so that the message is seen or acted out as well as heard. Turn the talk into a planned conversation or interview. With a small gathering, walk people around to focus on a particular window or even outside for a few minutes. Use ordinary household articles and everyday examples drawn from a variety of cultures and age groups so that everyone can empathise with at least one of the examples offered. Plan very carefully so that you don't drift about vaguely. Print out keywords and display them as you go to help people remember what they've heard.

The Credal statement

This is an opportunity for sometimes moving around the building, gathering around the font and using the water there as a reminder of Baptism, or an image of the life of Jesus in sculpture or windows. Celtic designs of the Trinity can be displayed, printed or projected. From time to time the statement of belief can be said with the right hand raised as an outward sign of commitment and dedication. Occasionally music can be played in the background as people speak out the words of their faith.

Prayers of intercession

As with the time of Penitence, sometimes give words a rest and go for projected images, sounds and music and symbols. Use the whole church building, setting up areas of prayer focus perhaps in front of a little-used high altar, in a side chapel or children's area or country church porch, with fabric, a globe, newspaper headlines and pictures, objects as symbols, charity magazine articles and suggested prayer concerns which reflect the focus of the day or the season. Have somewhere where people can light candles as they pray, or write or draw prayers on sticky notes. People can walk around on their own or with others, or they can sit or kneel in their places, and all age groups can then be involved in the fervent prayer of the gathered community.

The Eucharistic Prayer

Encourage those who can't see to gather round closer. Dress children as angels sometimes, with candles to hold. Project an image of the Last Supper, or of wheat and grapes. If you use real bread, involve different age groups in making it. The very fact that bread and wine are taken, blessed, broken and shared is, of course, wonderfully using the senses.

The Communion

Encourage reverence and quiet worship with the mood of music played. To adults not confirmed, and to baptised children who are not sharing the meal, give a candle as they are blessed, which they can go and light in a place of simple beauty.

Multi-layering

Differentiation by outcome

Much of the time, in the kind of worship I am suggesting for the gathered community, differentiation for the differing needs comes from a multi-sensory approach, and the expectation that people will be able to respond collectively, but in a variety of ways appropriate to particular ages and personalities. So following a reading, for instance, which everyone has heard communally, there might be a time allocated for everyone to respond, but with a variety of ways available to do this – perhaps through individual drawing, a group collage, making notes and underlining copies of the text, sitting quietly and reading it through again, looking at related images, or talking quietly together in small groups. All over the church there is a sense of engagement with a common theme, and yet there is enough flexibility to provide for the differences of personality, experience and faith development, as well as age differences.

It may well come as a surprise to find that when such a multi-layered response is offered, the chosen responses cut right across the traditional boundaries of age-group, so that a toddler and a grandparent might be working together on a drawing of the stormy sea being stilled by Jesus, a few young and elderly people are discussing together how Jesus manages to calm the storms in our lives, some children and adults are making a collage of a storm as they talk about how it might have felt for the disciples in the boat, and other people of all ages are sitting thinking and praying, on their own or in twos and threes, with the scripture passage in front of them, covered in underlining and asterisks.

Another example of this multi-layering is when a reading, hymn, mime, sketch or image, which is communally experienced, speaks to the gathered community on a variety of levels. The obvious example is in receiving Communion – a meal shared where Jesus is present among his people. Depending on who we are, where we are on our journey of faith, and what our experience has been during the past week, that 'touching place' will hold different treasures for everyone, feeding us all according to our needs.

Other facets of worship work in a similar way. Suppose there is a mime, for instance, which shows individuals cut off from one another, and all separately engaged in work which is exhausting them and preventing them from noticing one another's needs. One of the group finally notices Jesus' offer of help and draws the others into a communal sharing of the work, bringing fulfilment and freedom. For some people such a mime may help unpack a previous scripture reading about attentiveness to God. For some it will reinforce the value of sharing and helping one another, and for some it may raise questions or challenges about a particular situation at home or at work or in the church. An image can be used in the same way, speaking practically to some, inspirationally or symbolically to others. Hymns can work through mood, melody and particular phrases, just as much as through understanding all the language intellectually.

It isn't our business to dictate response, or narrow down the possibilities, but simply to provide a landscape of encounter, which allows God the space and opportunity to meet with people as they worship and touch their hearts and minds. The danger is that in largely word-centred liturgy, with its prescriptive nature, we can hijack the holy spaces of worship, till churches cease to be the places people think of coming to for spiritual help and enlightenment. Multi-layering is not about entertainment with a U-certification, but about real encounter with God from wherever you happen to be at the moment.

Practical caring

Worship is about honouring both God's 'worth' and the worth of one another. That means a well-earthed, practical attitude to everyone's needs and comforts. We have talked a great deal about accessibility in whole community worship, and we need to hear in that 'accessibility' word the challenges. Is the place of worship accessible to everyone, or are some excluded simply because they are wheelchair/stroller users, wobbly on steps, hearing- or sight-impaired, hyperactive, weak-bladdered, epileptic, or with special educational needs?

Part of providing a landscape for worship is taking a straight look at facilities offered and improving them where necessary. Often this is not a hopelessly expensive enterprise. Quite apart from the possibility of grants for public places, the difficulties can often be addressed by people willing to help in a friendly way, with everyone looking after the needs of one another.

Forgive me for stating the obvious, but I have so often been amazed by a supposedly Christian group of people in a church who stand pointedly looking straight ahead – often disapprovingly – while a young family struggles to cope with the needs of several children, one of whom needs the toilet, and others a bit of attention! You feel God's exaspera-tion ('How long have I been with you!?') with a people who have presumably never been taught that loving support and encouragement is all part of worshipping in spirit and in truth.

I know the child safety issues sometimes terrify us into denying compassion, and going for the avoidance option instead, but if this is true, perhaps we need to look afresh at some of the hidden costs of a child safety approach gone crazy. Utterly scrupulous care of both our children and adults is, of course, paramount, but I wonder if that is often achieved better by a watchful and loving community, with natural compassion and trust, than by a rule-bound fear of litigation where all human touch, even in public, is outlawed.

Another area of practical care is in recognising what people can cope with and what they can't. Babies and toddlers, for instance, are not going to be able to take full part in everything in a sustained way, any more than they would be expected to sit up to the table for the whole of a family celebration meal. They need to be able to 'get down from the table' from time to time, joining in again as they can. And that means providing a place within the church that is warm and friendly and safe – a nice place to be so that they look forward to coming. Part of worship for them is experiencing, in the loving and the security, the loving faithfulness of God.

So visit your existing children's area and imagine what you'd feel like using it. Is it kept clean and interesting, with quality activities available? (A rota for this care-taking role eases the strain.) There is plenty of scope for toys and activities related to the faith story – building bricks, dressing-up clothes, farmyards, Noah's arks, flocks of knitted sheep to look after, and 'creation' blankets with pockets containing stars, moon and planets, for example. Look at the secular market and be imaginative about adapting patterns and ideas. What about a 'Nazareth home' corner with clothes to dress up in and appropriate household items, such as bedrolls, playdough, brooms and brushes, and cooking pots, with a hobby-donkey outside? What about an area of water play sometimes? Or parable boxes with secrets inside, to help you tell yourself or your grandma the familiar stories?

For those playing with the children this becomes a gracious part of worship, and needs to be seen as that, rather than 'taking the children off everyone's hands'. Encourage parents to teach their children what worship is about by such involvement with them in celebrating God's loving kindness, truth and acceptance.

Drama

I think worship has always been of a dramatic nature. I don't mean that in the sense of being emotionally over the top, or in any way false. I mean that to be mortal and human, engaging in relationship by invitation with the Creator of the entire universe, is something so awe-inspiring and deep that we cannot help reacting with hushed voices, falling to our knees, lifting our hands, quietening into those profound silences, singing our hearts out in praise, or signing our own bodies with the sign of the cross.

Never mind the differences in style and tradition – it is simply a dramatic event that God Almighty should grace us with his presence and be there among us as a friend. Create an atmosphere which speaks of the holy and gives enough space for people to touch base with their soul, and the real drama will happen – lives being healed and transformed; the grace to forgive setting people free; hope sprouting up out of the muddy negative grumbling. It will happen because God longs for it to be so.

And what about using acting and mime in order to bring to life a reading from the Bible, or as a way of teaching, or exploring the depth of God's nature? It can certainly be very effective, in the sense that people can be drawn into the reality of an event so they are more easily touched by it. Using a dramatised Bible cuts down on the need to work out your own scripting, and costumes are a sensible resource to have available. Clipboards have a kind of 'invisible' quality about them, easily overlooked, so lines don't need to be learnt as long as they are well prepared by the readers.

If a passage is being narrated, accompanied by mime, it can often work better to do this unrehearsed, since the actors are responding freshly to the narration, and can be given stage directions where necessary as the reading progresses. The narrator simply has two different voice levels for this, rather as if they are speaking in brackets for any stage direc-tions. Developing a reading from scratch like this becomes part of the worship, and speaks to us about the preparation being all part of the act of love; of the journey being all part of the destination, as far as the kingdom is concerned.

Short sketches, both verbalised and mimed, are an excellent way of homing in on a truth far more quickly and effectively than lots of words. The humour and sharpness or immediacy of a sketch goes straight in to enlighten or challenge, and young people are often particularly gifted at this.

Liturgy

Worshipping as a whole community can work with any church tradition, and both Eucharistic and non-Eucharistic. It is all a question of thinking imaginatively and holistically, involving the physical, mental, spiritual and emotional, with sensitivity to the needs of all those present. Common Worship provides a very useful format for a Service of the Word, either with or without a celebration of Holy Communion, which leaves us plenty of freedom to plan, and there are all kinds of alternative ways available for the different sections of the liturgy. Do familiarise yourself with them and try them out.

As the Introduction to 'A Service of the Word' makes clear, this kind of liturgy 'consists almost entirely of notes and directions and allows for considerable local variation and choice within a common structure'. I often meet with a scepticism about such liturgy among 'purists', who cannot believe that it could really hold together graciously and with enough sense of awe and reverence. Others are scared to plunge into something so spacious, feeling insecure because of the lack of a handrail.

If you haven't experienced anything like this before, allow me to put some of those fears to rest and encourage you. There is still quite a clear structure – it's just more light-weight, like a cloister rather than a corridor. There is often actually more opportunity for those leading to take part in the worship experience, since the spaces with music and image do not need anyone taking the lead at that point. As when friends are invited round for a meal, the cook sits down with the guests and everyone shares time and conversation and food together. The other point is that a sense of order and reverence comes about through order and reverence in the planning. We are to fill our water pots with water, and it is Jesus who changes the water into wine.

Here are some general liturgical guidelines for priests and ministers to bear in mind:

- Keep things simple.
- Worship in humility yourself, the whole time you are leading others in worship.
- Clear instructions as you go will not interrupt the flow!
- Where you don't need words, don't use them.
- Vary the type of activity throughout the worship time.
- Provide space.
- Relax in God's company.
- Enjoy the time of worship together.
- Be both well-organised and flexible.
- Resist the temptation to control, dominate or empire-build – this is all about God's kingdom, not yours.
- Listen to people of all ages, seeking out their opinions, noticing how their faith is growing.
- Those who speak loudly and negatively are probably not as representative as they claim. Check out the true picture, and don't be bullied.
- Be yourself. God called you that way.

In conclusion . . .

Always remember why you are doing what you are doing. If ever the thing itself takes over in importance from the primary call to worship God, be courageous in recognising that this has happened, and pull it back into its proper place. Never let it squeeze its way on to the throne of God. Try not to get in God's way, but allow him access. He is, after all, the reason we are there!

Using an OHP creatively

Traditionally an overhead projector has been used either educationally as a kind of blackboard, or as a communal hymnsheet. With video projectors and PowerPoint visual presentations still out of budget for most churches, the humble overhead projector can still open up for us many creative possibilities for worship. It's just a question of thinking imaginatively and trying out ideas. Here are a few to start you off:

- Print colour or black and white images on to clear inkjet film to make your own library of colour transparencies for worship.
- Fade an image before you print it so as to hint at a mood, and layer this with the words of a hymn.
- Print a short prayer or soundbite from a reading and layer this with an image, lining it up to be in a light area of the picture – such as the sunlight or sky.
- Use the projector as a shadow box, placing cut-out silhouettes directly on the light plate. They will be projected sharply in focus. You can move these around as you talk. Build up a library of such symbols and characters.
- Use actual objects in the same way as a focus for prayer, or as part of instruction.
- Place a glass dish on the light plate, and pour water into it. Colour the water, put bubbles in it, or place one of those fizzing bath balls in it so the bubbles stream out.
- Place coloured gauze or lace as a background. Experiment with different textures.
- Make 'stained glass window' pictures with coloured tissue or, even better, coloured film in an opaque frame.
- Use glass paints to colour outline pictures you have printed out. (Leave white areas blank as the white glass paint is opaque.)
- Place a blank film on the light plate and write or draw as people watch.
- Print a black outline on one film, and then colour and decorate a second – the word LIFE for instance. The plain one can be projected first on its own and then in all its possible brightness.
- Use three films all based on the same word – GOD – to explore visually the Persons of the Trinity.

A walk through the seasons

Having looked at the reasons behind this kind of whole-community worship, at some of the basic principles to bear in mind, and in more detail at the practicalities of it, I think it may be helpful to run our hands over the shape of a year. It's a question of walking out of the trees for a while and climbing a hill to view the whole forest from a distance. So first you may like to read through all the seasonal introductions as a whole, before returning to a particular season, rereading the introduction and then following the suggestions for each particular Sunday.

Seeing the shape of the year like this will help us plan worship which picks up on the mood of the year's seasons, which Common Worship celebrates so well. The great advantage of following the Church year is that we get a rounded, balanced diet, and plenty of variety within the familiarity of pattern. The year's cycle gives balance and stability to our worship, a healthy, all-round diet of reflection and celebration, light and shade, the challenging, the comforting and the inspiring. It ensures that as a church we don't risk focusing so much on one area of our faith that others are ignored. In a sense it is all one year-long or life-long service, and by worshipping together week by week throughout a complete year the church is fed.

Broadly speaking, there are the two chunks of 'real time' around Christmas and Easter, which encourage us to tell the story in a Passover way of reliving as we retell, and the rest of the year exploring in different ways the nature of God and the extraordinary plan of salvation. The Church year begins not on 1 January but four Sundays before Christmas, round about the start of December.

But each year has a different Gospel flavour. Recognising and celebrating the different viewpoints and styles of the Gospels, the readings give us a Year of Matthew, of Mark and of Luke. After a great deal of discussion it was decided that, rather than having a separate fourth Year of John, John's Gospel was needed in every year, so this Gospel is not left out, but incorporated into the other three years, which again ensures a balance of style, emphasis and viewpoint. Rather than an identikit picture of Jesus, with the Gospels merged and differences blurred, the provision of these yearly flavours encourage us as a community to hear the voice of each evangelist telling the story in their own way – and it is a good idea for churches to have a straight public 'read-through' of each Gospel on a regular basis.

The season of Advent

The four weeks before Christmas Day are called Advent (The Coming) because the Church focuses on the coming of Christ to the world, both as a baby in Bethlehem about 2000 years ago and also at the completion of all things, as our Judge and King.

So it is a time of individual and collective preparation and expectancy as we focus on those 'end things' of such deep importance for us. We are watching and waiting, doing some honest soul-searching, living through the bustle of pre-Christmas with a rather wider agenda than presents, tinsel and turkey. It is as if, deep in the heart of us as God's People, there is in Advent an insistent and urgent drumbeat, summoning us to be watchful and attentive to what God has done, is doing and will do.

The repetition I have suggested in some simple actions, words and symbols over the Advent season helps us focus together on the Advent themes as distinct from the festivities of Christmas, and provides us with space to wonder, so that when Christmas comes it is like the full light of dawn breaking and filling the dark earth with God's shining love.

The colour is purple, to catch this mood of soul-searching and penitence as we face up to the enormity of God's plan for us. In the season of Advent, as darkness advances on the hours of daylight, there is a wonderfully contrasting sense of gradually unfolding hope and growing light, which has been carefully traced in the lectionary, and we can emphasise this in our liturgy.

Use the purple colour

Have purple streamers for the children to worship with in the times of singing, and a couple of Advent flags in the same colour range. Choose purple fabric as the basis for prayer areas.

Advent wreaths with a difference

Usually those five candles are already in place, with an extra one lit each week. Another way of using the wreath is to start on Advent Sunday with none of the candles on it. The first lit candle is processed through the church during the first reading – perhaps by a young person dressed in a white garment.

For each week of Advent another candle is carried through the church in procession to join those already lit, so that the link between prophecy and growing enlightenment is visually made. An alternative way of doing this is to have one candle brought in procession the first week, two the second, and so on, so that the accumulating brightness is there in the procession as well as on the wreath.

Soundbites of the season

The words of Isaiah 2:5 can become a soundbite for this season of expectation and journey. Children can draw around their feet and write the words on their footprints, which are then taped to the aisle floor, so that everyone walks past them on their way to receive Communion, or on their way out of church.

The words might be used as part of the invitation to confession or as the response to the prayers of intercession. They might be written near or around the Advent wreath, and as a heading for the pew sheet. Everyone can then join in with them during the reading on the first Sunday of Advent. They can be written in bubble writing on a length of lining paper, which the very young children can decorate with crayons or stuck-on pieces of shiny wrapping paper during the talk or sermon.

Opening windows through Advent

The custom of Advent calendars can be more than simply a countdown to Christmas Day. 'Opening windows' during the weeks of Advent, to reveal to us more of what it means for Christ to come among us, is a valuable way of involving the whole church community in celebrating this season. It isn't difficult to prepare, as you are simply adding to the calendars many people have already. Encourage every home to get a calendar this year.

Using the lectionary Sunday readings, choose the daily Bible references you want the whole church to share (see Resources, page 113) and write these references on a sheet of paper, with copies for every household. Whenever people open their various Advent calendar windows at home they also read the chosen verse, so that the calendar becomes a focus for prayer, and the window is opening not just to a Christmas picture or a chocolate, but to fresh understanding of God's unfolding plan of salvation.

Preparing for the coming of the Servant King

It is no accident that the Sunday immediately before Advent is celebrated as 'Christ the King'. Even as we acknowledge Jesus as the One worthy to receive all honour and glory, we recognise also the humility of his servanthood, willingly taken, out of love for us all.

Advent stretches us immediately into thinking in two dimensions at once – forward to the end of time and Jesus' coming in glory, and backward to the tracing of the clues leading to a human baby wrapped in cloths in the straw. Both the 'Servant' and the 'King' themes are here to reflect on in this season of shadowy darkness and flickering light.

So, where you might normally have a flower arrangement during other seasons, arrange for a still life to be created each Sunday of Advent during the service. You might have a towel, jug and bowl, with a crown and some draped velvet or brocade. During the Creed, have age group representatives bringing the different items from all over the church, and arranging them on the fabric. Then a cross is placed in the centre, and the words: 'Then they will see the Son of Man . . .'

First Sunday of Advent, Years ABC

Focus of the service: Watching and waiting. The patriarchs.
Mood: Expectant. Honest. Time to wake up and get ready.

Possibilities for worship:

- The words from the day's reading (such as Isaiah 2:5: 'Come, let us walk in the light of the Lord!') printed in bubble writing, with crayons and pens available.
- Paper, crayons, scissors and tape for drawing round feet, writing words from the readings and taping to the floor.
- Purple streamers and flags available to wave in worship during hymns.
- Instruments ready for accompanying the last hymn.
- CDs reflecting the mood and focus as people gather, during the time of Penitence and Intercessions.
- Projected images of winter trees in a cold landscape; of the dawn; of people and animals in harmony to focus on during the time of Penitence.
- Lighting the first of the Advent candles (see page 29 for ideas).
- Arrange the Old Testament passage to be read by different voices, with some verses by everyone.

Areas of prayer focus around the church:

- Use purple fabric.
- A collection of clocks and watches and calendars, among pictures and headlines of concern, with verses chosen from the day's readings, together with the following: 'Give us grace to cast off the works of darkness and to put on the armour of light' (Collect for the day).

Second Sunday of Advent, Years ABC

Focus of the service: The whole world waiting in hope. The prophets help us get ready.
Mood: Hopeful, expectant, listening and attentive.

Possibilities for worship:

- Purple streamers and flags.
- Projected images of road building; of people from different cultures; of dawn.
- A font full of water, or several bowls of water around the church, with hand towels, for a time of penitence and affirmation of God's forgiveness. Give people time to come and wash their hands if they would like to.
- Read the Old Testament passage split verse by verse with men and boys, and women and girls.
- Pick a verse or phrase from the day's readings that jumps out at you, to be copied ready for tracing, decorating and displaying. Provide coloured pencils and pens.
- Recorded music from a different area of the world, and a globe prominent as people come into church, with an appropriate text (Year A: 'Let all the peoples praise him'; Year B: 'Then the glory of the Lord shall be revealed, and all people shall see it together'; Year C: 'All flesh shall see the salvation of God').
- Act out the Gospel, in script form, or miming to narration. John the Baptist might be dressed up, even in a token way.
- The second Advent candle is lit.

Areas of prayer focus around the church:

- Purple fabric.
- Pictures of people of all ages and cultures crying and being comforted; water with floating candles; globes or world maps. Phrases to direct people's prayers – 'Pray for better listening'; 'Pray for those who don't know God loves them'; 'Pray for those who have lost hope'; and so on.

Third Sunday of Advent, Years ABC

Focus of the service: God is coming in person to save us. John the Baptist as the herald.

Mood: Excitement and joy are building, as the hope of the kingdom gets closer.

Possibilities for worship:
- Purple and silver streamers.
- Projected images of majestic landscapes or skyscapes; of water; of an open gate or door.
- Recorded music which catches the mood of the day.
- Prime different people or groups of people to take part in the gospel, not coming out together at the front to start with, but shouting from their places, or coming from their seats as they speak.
- Stage an interview with John the Baptist.
- The third Advent candle is lit.

Areas of prayer focus around the church:
- Use both purple and white or gold fabric
- Phrases to encourage prayers of thanksgiving for God's goodness and loving care; pictures of natural wonders, people's faces; phrases from the readings as encouragement.

Fourth Sunday of Advent, Years ABC

Focus of the service: The promised kingdom of God's reign will last for ever. Mary agrees to be part of the plan
Mood: Wonder and hope; growing expectation; excitement.

Possibilities for worship:
- Purple, pink and silver for streamers, flags and so on.
- The fourth Advent candle is lit – have someone dressed as Mary to do this, with everyone joining in her words to Gabriel: 'Here I am, the servant of the Lord. Let it be with me as you have said.'
- Project images of paintings of the annunciation from a variety of cultures and times at different points of the service.
- Use paintings or stained glass windows in the church as a focus for the meditation, prayers or talk (you don't have to agree with the artist's viewpoint – make it a conversation or discussion time).
- Act out the Gospel reading, with costumes.
- Have a 'Here I am, the servant of the Lord' basket and invite people to write their signature on small pieces of paper and 'sign up' to the statement at the offertory or before the service.

Areas of prayer focus around the church:
- Use purple or pink cloths with some silver, to suggest the Advent season being lit by the light of Christmas this week.
- Have a lily at each prayer focus with Mary's words.
- Use pictures and stories from the Christmas Charity appeals to highlight needs.
- Print suggestions for prayer: 'Pray for those who are dreading Christmas'; 'Pray that Jesus may be born in our hearts and lives'; 'Pray for those faced with big decisions to make'; 'Pray for the grace to tell others about God's love for us all'.

The season of Christmas

The time of waiting and preparation has come to an end. The Church, out of step with the Christmassy December of the high street, struggles to hold on to this waiting, and in doing so is a sign of a deep truth about our need to wait on God expectantly. The longer Christmas is held off the better! Sometimes, of course, we have to live in both seasons at once, but if we can manage to keep an awareness of Advent alive even through all the carol services, there is a different feel to Christmas itself.

At the first service of Christmas – often in darkness – the celebration is of God at a particular moment in history, being born into humanness, entering by birth the narrow gateway we have all shared, from the darkness of the womb into the light of life. No wonder everyone senses the deep magic of this extraordinary event – the utterly natural lit by the unnervingly mystical.

Encountering God among us is what all our worship is about, so the Incarnation is our opportunity to marvel afresh at what is at the heart of all our worship – God's presence in person. Instinctively we reach for candlelight, bells and any-thing that reflects light – like the very tinsel we despise as a byword for rubbish values. Yet in fact the sense of light touching different surfaces and turning them into light is a valid reminder of how Jesus' coming lights up our lives, so perhaps those high street decorations have more value than we think.

Christmas is a time when worship is somehow acceptable and even welcomed, with people still drawn to worship in churches. They might well find it embarrassing or unnatural to engage with the 'churchiness', but something draws them to touch base, hoping and daring to experience the special, the mystical, the 'otherness' of God. Perhaps they are hoping to find 'thin' places where God's presence brushes against the humanness and lights it up.

Catching the holiness

Use the natural as the touchstone of holiness. Candle flames, focused lighting, glinting surfaces, silence, enveloping organ music which then guides us down into quietness. Hushed voices speaking together, singing together. Space for personal response and reflection while others sing. A crib scene which allows us to imagine stepping into the event ourselves, and opportunity to wonder and marvel, 're-membering' the child-like in us. Use gold or white streamers and coloured flags.

Christmas spirit of generosity

Not surprisingly, everyone finds themselves thinking 'lavish generosity' at Christmas. Let the worship reflect this generous giving, making it all part of the service – a celebration and festival of our giving, like at Harvest, when giving is once again our natural, human response to God's gifts. Make the giving fun. Decorated boxes for toiletries and food and toys. Information and pictures of where the gifts will be used. Communal Christmas cards linked with a collection of saved money for a particular charity. All ages involved in the decorating, the flowers and the cleaning. Transport offered for those finding it hard to come.

Awe and wonder

The Christchild enables us all to remember our own wonder of birth, together with the vulnerability of our mortal humanness, as we look at the disturbingly vulnerable nature of God. Here is God baby-sized and dependent but at the same time small enough to be manageable and in our control. So Christmas worship must help us hold on to the transcendent, even as we focus on the immanent. Use recorded music, carol singing and candles. Have a real mother and baby and a bale of hay.

Encourage the questions

The consequence of our cultural shift of Christmas back into Advent is that by the Sunday after Christmas we are totally partied out! However, that presents us with an opportunity to tune in to our natural inclination for practical 'packing up' of Christmas in the two weeks of the season by exploring some of the practical implications of an incarnate God regarding the place we know as home – both our human households and also in the vast created universe we inhabit. Have a question box and dip into it. Write some of the questions large, and place them around the church, so people can ponder them and write their thoughts on flipcharts as part of a sermon slot.

During the Christmas season our worship of the Christchild leads us deeper into an understanding not only of who God is but also of who we are. The wonder can lead us into the big questions, and the questions lead us into a fresh and God-given self-awareness.

Christmas Day, Years ABC

Focus of the service: The Lord of heaven and earth is born as a human baby.

Mood: Joy. Celebration. Awe and wonder. Sense of mystery.

Possibilities for worship:

- Have the baby Jesus figure carried round to the crib by a dressed 'nativity play' procession, or in a robed procession by the president.
- Silver, gold and white streamers and flags.
- Projected images of the nativity taken from Christmas cards.
- Have a living crib to gather around as you sing a carol, at the Gospel, and the Creed.
- Give out bells to be rung at the Gloria – and party poppers if that feels appropriate.
- Children dressed as angels hold candles around the altar during the Eucharistic Prayer
- CD of magical, wonder-ful music such as the *Nutcracker Suite*, *Harry Potter* film soundtrack or *The Snowman*.
- Soundbites: 'The Word became flesh and dwelt among us'; 'And she gave birth to her firstborn son'; 'Wonderful Counsellor, Mighty God, the Everlasting Father, the Prince of Peace'.

Areas of prayer focus around the church:

- Gold, silver and white fabric.
- Star shapes to write prayers on.
- Christmas cards among the suggestions for prayer.
- Prayer suggestions: 'Teach us about real peace'; 'Pray for families celebrating together'; 'Pray for those who find this a difficult time'; 'Jesus, I love you'.

First Sunday of Christmas, Years ABC

Focus of the service: Jesus growing up in his family: Mary, Joseph and Jesus. The practical implications of Incarnation start to show.
Mood: Still festive. Lots of celebration, but also reflective.

Possibilities for worship:

- Silver, gold and white for streamers or flags.
- Give out bells and triangles for playing in one or two carols.
- 'Glory to God in the Highest!' projected against an image of creation's glory, with the organ playing out praise, and everyone clapping, ringing bells, waving streamers and flags, or silent and still in worship.
- The Gospel acted out – a mixed aged group – in costume.
- A live baby wrapped and held by Mum dressed as Mary during the Old Testament reading (Years A and B).
- A young boy in a white robe walking up and down the church, holding hands with his mother during the Old Testament reading (Year C).
- Verses from Psalm 148 printed out in bubble writing for colouring and illustrating.

Areas of prayer focus around the church:

- Silver, gold and white fabric.
- Mirrors with tea-light candles on them to light.
- Pictures from different cultures of children and their parents.
- Suggestions for prayer: 'Pray for those being born this week'; 'Pray that all children may be safe and well loved'; 'Pray for parents'; 'Pray for families who have had to leave their homes'; 'Pray for families living in fear and danger'; 'Give us the grace to forgive one another'; 'Give us the grace to love one another'.

Second Sunday of Christmas, Years ABC

Focus of the service: The Word became flesh and dwelt among us. The Incarnation.
Mood: Thoughtful and thankful. Wonder at God's love and humility.

Possibilities for worship:

- Mysterious and 'this is bigger than we can ever understand' kind of music on CD or organ, such as *Lord of the Rings*, or Mahler, as people are coming in.
- White, silver and gold for streamers and flags.
- Projected images of cosmic beauty – stars and nebula, dramatic skyscapes, close-up of a baby's hands.
- A candle held high during the Gospel.
- The Gloria shout (see page 114).
- Everyone holding their breath for a few seconds to experience the 'now' and God in person among us.
- Set out the Gospel to be read by different voices – men and boys together, women and girls together, perhaps a single child's voice for verse 18, carefully rehearsed.
- Soundbite printed out large for communal colouring, or written out on calendar pictures of creation.

Areas of prayer focus around the church:

- Silver, gold and white fabric.
- Today's soundbite printed out for each area.
- A bowl of water and floating candle.
- Images of light and darkness and shadows.
- Prayer suggestions: 'Thank God for all your blessings'; 'Thank God for his love and humility'; 'Pray for the world to welcome him'; 'Pray for those who don't know God'; 'Pray for those who are still waiting for the Christ to come'.

The season of Epiphany

A season of revelation follows naturally on from the birth of Christ. We begin with the journeying of the wise men who search to find the child of all wisdom, and this starts us too on a journey of discovery, where Jesus is gradually revealed as the Son of God, the promised and awaited Messiah, or Christ.

The season engages with the question 'Who is this Jesus?' and answers with hints, signs and clues, recognising how expectations and preconceptions colour our sight and affect our discernment. Travelling through the season as the wise men travelled – with commitment, expectancy and openness – we too can behold his glory as of the only begotten of the Father, full of grace and truth. Reflecting on the Gospel stories of Christ's true nature being revealed brings us each year to a fresh discovery of God's presence in our lives.

The Epiphany season, and in fact the whole sweep of Advent, Christmas and Epiphany, culminates in the festival of Candlemas, where the six-week-old infant Jesus is brought into the temple at Jerusalem. Here is God's Son entering the house of the Lord in all the candour, simplicity and vulnerability of a young baby carried in his mother's arms. The story is prophetic, with the child acting out, in this traditional ceremony for Jewish families, nothing less than God returning to dwell among his people in person. And will anyone notice?

As all the other stories of the season have shown us, to the open and expectant, Christ is revealed. Simeon and Anna have been waiting their lifetime – waiting attentive and patient and prepared to be surprised. So now they are able to see in what is happening the way God is acting. They can sense the full force of the story behind and within the event.

Simeon's words of prophecy turn us both back to the baby born in Bethlehem and also forward to the shadow of the cross. Love is the fulfilling of the Law, and Love hurts.

Our Epiphany worship needs to pick up on the questions, the expectations, the humility and obedience and, above all, on the revealed nature of Christ. There needs to be an ongoing sense of journey, discovery and openness to God, practical help with the patient waiting on God, and celebration at the revelation, broken free of geography and nationalism, given to the whole world.

Stars   Have some constellations of stars displayed, star-shaped paper for people to write their prayers on, stars printed on service sheets, stars with Bible references about who Jesus is, taped to the floor and walls.

Questions   Continue the question box through Epiphany, so people can write their questions and have them answered and discussed.

Signs   Collect signs and symbols week by week (perhaps water and the dove, a key for Jesus unlocking the secrets of God, a jug of water and wedding wine glasses, and a picture of an eye for God being all-seeing and all-knowing). Arrange question marks around them, so that the continuity of the season is kept in people's minds, even if they miss a Sunday or two.

Have the raised letters of WHAT IS GOD LIKE? and JESUS SHOWS US WHAT GOD IS LIKE under a sheet of lining paper with crayons available so anyone can add to the rubbing of it and reveal the message.

The Epiphany, Years ABC

Focus of the service: Jesus is revealed to the whole world. The wise men visit Jesus. Searching and being shown.
Mood: Festive. A sense of our own search and journey.

Possibilities for worship:

- Display the gifts – something gold (or chocolate money), a bowl of incense burning (or an incense stick), and a spice jar of myrrh (or a pot of soothing ointment) with labels for each: 'the One we honour as King', 'the One we worship as God', 'the Great Healer'.

- Accompany the Old Testament reading with music which has a sense of dawn (such as 'Morning' from Grieg's *Peer Gynt Suite*. All the children and some carers gather from all over the church in verse 4.

- Act out the Gospel with costumes, giving the wise men as long a journey as possible.

- Have the wise men models moving week by week towards the crib and now they join it just before or just after the Gospel.

- Use the gifts as a focus for penitence – gold of obedience, incense of lowliness or reverence, myrrh of healing and comforting.

- Soundbite: 'And they offered him their gifts – gold, frankincense and myrrh.'

Areas of prayer focus around the church:

- Gold and blue fabric.

- Globe and compass.

- Bowl of incense, gold crown, myrrh.

- Suggestions for prayer: 'Pray for those who have lost their way'; 'Pray for all who are seeking truth and meaning in their lives'; 'Guide our steps through life, Lord God'; 'Teach us your wisdom'; 'May you be known in all the world'.

The Baptism of Christ: First Sunday of Epiphany, Years ABC

Focus of the service: Jesus is baptised both in water by John and by the Holy Spirit of God. Our own baptism.

Mood: Watchful and attentive as God shows us what he is doing in Jesus.

Possibilities for worship:

- White, silver and blue streamers to walk in through.
- CD of sounds of water – ocean surf or running river – as background to the gospel reading.
- Images of water projected – shore and waves, droplets and reflections.
- Use the font as a focus for penitence, splashing everyone with water as the words of God's forgiveness are proclaimed.
- Have a group of mixed ages reading the Old Testament passage chorally.
- Use different voices for conversation in the readings.
- Gather round the font for the Gospel, and have a floating candle on the water.
- Have soundbites from today's readings written with candles on paper, and provide blue watery paint to brush on, so the words are gradually revealed.

Areas of prayer focus around the church:

- White, silver and blue cloth.
- Water with stones and shells.
- Suggestions for prayer printed on separate pieces of card among pictures of water.
- Prayer suggestions: 'Pray for all who have been baptised'; 'Make us worthy of our calling'; 'Pray for God's love to pour into your heart'; 'Pray for someone you long to know Jesus better'; 'Pray for all who are thirsty'.

Second Sunday of Epiphany, Years ABC

Focus of the service: The identity of Jesus is revealed to those who are looking.
Mood: Personal involvement with Jesus. 'This is for real' challenge. Attentive. Curious.

Possibilities for worship:

- White, silver, gold. A sense of wedding party for Year C.
- CD of wedding music (Year C) and a sense of a hidden mystery being revealed (Years A and B) such as *The Planets* by Holst, the theme from *2001: A Space Odyssey*, or Sibelius.
- Projected images of question marks (all different sizes and styles, cut from thin card, using OHP as shadow box).
- Have an image of Christ, or the words 'You are the Christ!', covered and gradually uncovered, either on the floor or projected.
- For the time of Penitence, focus on what we usually try to hide from others and from God – cup hands as if you are holding something inside. Peer into the dark space so only you can see. Tell God you are sorry and want to be forgiven and freed. Open up your hands and let God take from you the things you have kept hidden.
- One or two painters have long strips of lining paper fixed to the wall or on the floor, on which they interpret the focus of Jesus being revealed as the Son of God.

Areas of prayer focus around the church:

- White, silver, gold cloth.
- Years A and B: have arrows from question marks to an exclamation mark; Year C: flowers, glasses, ribbons.
- Images of particular needs from the local area and worldwide, headlines from newspapers, and photographs of local situations.
- Suggestions for prayer printed out separately and placed among the images: 'Do whatever he tells you'; 'Help us to recognise your voice and follow you day by day'; 'Pray for those who are sensing your call'; 'Pray for those trying their best not to hear your voice'; 'Pray that Christians may not block God's way'.

Third Sunday of Epiphany, Years ABC

Year A: Calling of first disciples
Year B: First 'sign' at wedding
Year C: First sermon of ministry

Focus of the service: By words and signs Jesus starts announcing the kingdom.
Mood: Challenging. Vocational. Dramatic.

Possibilities for worship:

- A trumpet or bugle to play like a herald before the service and before the gospel.
- Year A: Jesus calling out his gospel message walking up the aisle.
- Year A: project a picture of Galilee, and play sounds of the sea as a background to the reading. The prophet Isaiah reads that section from a scroll (verses 15-16).
- Year B: create a wedding atmosphere with flowers, glasses and ribbon.
- Year C: have Jesus handed a scroll during the Gospel, and sitting down to read the words from Isaiah from it.
- Have a scribble wall of lining paper with crayons available, headed: 'What does Jesus show us about God's kingdom?' Writers should scribe for non-writers; drawing is also an excellent method of recording.
- A recording of Semitic wedding folk music could be playing as people come into church (Year B).

Areas of prayer focus around the church:

- Continue the theme of each year in the colours and 'feel' of the prayer areas.
- Soundbites from the Gospel printed out and arranged among images of a great variety of people pictures.
- 'Let your kingdom come!' with a crown and a folded towel at the centre of each area to remind people of the 'servant kingdom' we are called into.
- Prayer suggestions: 'Pray for those whose life has suddenly changed'; 'Pray that we may hear God's call and respond to it'; 'Pray for those who need the healing of God's love and forgiveness'; 'Pray for the grace to see people as God sees them'; 'Thank God for all the blessings in your life'.

Fourth Sunday of Epiphany, Years ABC

Focus of the service: Jesus is the challenging sign of God's authority and loving provision.
Mood: Awareness of the heavenly in the earthly. Awe and wonder. The reality of God's presence in the world we know.

Possibilities for worship:

- Year A: create a wedding atmosphere with white, silver and gold, flowers and ribbon streamers.
- Year B and C: images (both visual and descriptive) of dramatic power in nature.
- Sounds of nature, such as a storm, or the sea pounding.
- Projected images of nature's glory and power during the Creed, with music playing as a background to everyone speaking out the words with conviction.
- If you have a small congregation, invite everyone to come to the font and cup their hands. Pour water over their cupped hands so that it trickles through their fingers and out into the font. During this have someone reading or singing the day's psalm, which celebrates God's abundant provision.
- Use different voices for the Gospel reading. (Consider having someone placed within the congregation for the Year B reading, but don't make it so frightening that people are badly scared.)

Areas of prayer focus around the church:

- White, silver and gold fabric, flowers, vegetables and fruit, candles and a glass jug of water.
- Have a lamp and some separate arrows laid out to point towards a cross or an icon of Christ.
- Suggestions for prayer printed on separate cards: 'Open our eyes to see your glory each day this week'; 'Pray for those who are in great need'; 'Pray for those who have lost the joy of giving'; 'Give us not what we want but what we need'.

The Presentation of Christ in the Temple, Years ABC

Focus of the service: Jesus is presented in the temple. Simeon and Anna recognise him, and prophesy about his life being a Sign and a Light.

Mood: Looking both back to Christmas and forward to Holy Week and Easter. A distinct change of mood, with the shadow of the cross falling on the baby and his mother.

Possibilities for worship:

- Plenty of candlelight in a darkened church.
- Orange Christingles, with their symbolism of the light shining out over the world with all its fruits and seasons, circled by the saving love of Jesus.
- Project a painting of this Presentation event, such as Rembrandt's.
- Have a costumed tableau of this painting during the Gospel.
- The colour is silver and gold.
- Place a light behind a cross so that the shadow of a cross falls over the sanctuary.

Areas of prayer focus around the church:

- Have pictures of Christmas and Easter (perhaps from greetings cards) on each area.
- Choose soundbites from the Gospel and print them out separately, placing them among the prayer intentions.
- Include a lamp at each area.
- Prayer intentions: 'Give us the courage to seek the One True God'; 'Pray for the very young and their parents'; 'Pray God's light to shine in our world'; 'Thank God for all who have been faithful throughout their long lives'; 'Help us to recognise you in one another'.

Ordinary Time: the countdown to Lent

After all the drama and movement of Advent, Christmas and Epiphany, there is now a season of quiet reflection. The length of this time varies with the date of Easter, and it marks a change of mood as it leans towards Lent, Holy Week and Easter. We are also conscious of stepping off the chronological 'realtime' for a while.

It is like the three dots that traditionally suggest a passing of time, and we need this to put down the babyhood of Jesus before we rejoin the gospel narrative at the start of his public ministry.

In our worship we can reflect the mood of this season by putting away the symbols of Christmas and Epiphany, and having the signs of Lent and Easter visible but not yet unpacked.

Proper 1, Years ABC

*(Sunday between 3 and 9 February,
if earlier than Second Sunday before Lent)*

Focus of the service: Our commission to spread the good news by word and lives.
Mood: Awe and wonder leading to heightened sense of calling and responsibility.

Possibilities for worship:

- Have green streamers and flags available for hymns and Gloria.
- Focus on the wonder of the Isaiah reading, using music of mystery and wonder to accompany it, and using several voices, sometimes separately, sometimes together.
- Year A: use the images of salt and light, together with soundbites from the Gospel.
- Year B: images of people talking in groups, on the phone, etc., together with soundbites from the Gospel.
- Year C: fishing net, sand and shells, together with soundbites from the Gospel.

Areas of prayer focus around the church:

- Use green and silver fabric.
- Have water with floating candles.
- Have tiny arrangements of flowers and foliage in screwtop lids filled with oasis.
- Prayer suggestions: 'Here I am, Lord. Send me'; 'Open our ears to hear your call and give us courage to follow you'; 'Pray for all church leaders'; 'Pray that your church may be a living sign of God's truth and love'.

Proper 2, Years ABC

(Sunday between 10 and 16 February,
if earlier than second Sunday before Lent)

Focus of the service: Choosing the way of life, life in all its fullness.
Jesus fulfils the law.
Mood: Buoyant, surprising and challenging. A sense of something
new which is really an ancient truth revealed in its beauty and
costliness.

Possibilities for worship:

- Green and silver banners, flags and streamers.
- The Ten Commandments displayed large on one wall and the Summary of the Law on the opposite side.
- Year A: have two voices reading the Gospel, one taking the 'you have heard it said' sections and the other voice the 'but I . . .' sections.
- Year B: act out the Gospel with the healed leper walking about telling people in the pews about how he is healed.
- Year C: have two voices for the Gospel, one reading the 'blessed are you . . .' section and the other the balancing reason for blessing.
- Projected images of trees planted by water, open doors, gateways or ancient steps, lamplights and candles being lit.

Areas of prayer focus around the church:

- Green fabric.
- Year B: Information about those suffering from leprosy and AIDS.
- Pictures and headlines amongst soundbites from the Gospel and a torch and compass.
- Prayer suggestions: 'Pray for those with big or difficult decisions to make'; 'Pray for a healing and cleansing of our motives'; 'Pray for those needing God's grace to forgive someone'; 'Pray for all whose illnesses make them despised or rejected'.

Proper 3, Years ABC

*(Sunday between 17 and 23 February,
if earlier than Second Sunday before Lent)*

Focus of the service: Our calling to generous, forgiving love.
Mood: Challenging, penitential, inspiring.

Possibilities for worship:

- Green streamers and instruments available for times of praise.
- Give reflective space to the time of Penitence, using the senses. While music is played, give everyone two sticks so they can make the shape of a cross by 'crossing out' the 'I' of selfishness while recognising the selfishness in our individual lives and in our culture.
- Have these words printed out or projected: 'Love your enemies. Do good to those who hate you. Pray for those who hurt you.' Very quietly the congregation recites them six times. Above this hushed chanting of Jesus' teaching, three people from different parts of the church shout out their protests: 1. 'But you can't expect me to forgive them! Not after what they've done!' 2. 'It was terrible – unforgivable. How can I possibly love them now?' 3. 'But they've ruined my whole life. Why should I forgive them?' Leave enough space between each protest for the teaching to be heard through, and this teaching to be the last thing left in people's minds.
- Projected images of peaceful landscapes or seascapes, a close-up of hands shaking in 'making up', or a dog looking guilty!

Areas of prayer focus around the church:

- Green fabric.
- Have small vases of water in each area and a bowl of cut flowers and foliage available. Suggest that as people pray they take a flower and place it in the vase where they have prayed.
- Prayer suggestions: 'Pray for those who are finding it very hard to forgive'; 'Pray for the grace to forgive and to accept that we are forgiven'; 'Pray for nations and states at war'; 'Pray for your enemies and any who curse or insult you'; 'Forgive us our trespasses as we forgive those who trespass against us'.
- In between the prayer suggestions and vases of flowers have pictures and headlines from the newspapers and any charity or aid magazines which highlight particular needs.

Second Sunday before Lent, Years ABC

Focus of the service: The loving Lord of all creation is shown in person in Jesus.
Mood: Getting in touch with who we are and where we come from. Wonder and thankfulness. Trust in the God who made us.

Possibilities for worship:

- Green, white and blue streamers – land and sea and sky colours.
- Projected images of sea and landscapes and the beauty of creation, and of question marks of different sizes and styles.
- Natural sounds – birdsong or ocean or running streams.
- Length of lining paper with crayons and the words 'Lord of all creation' in bubble writing on it for anyone to draw, colour or write in the bits of creation they enjoy.
- Rubbings of the word 'Love' available to make (with the letters in thick card placed under paper and scribbled over with coloured wax crayons).
- Year C: act out the Gospel – or have lengths of blue/green cloth flapped gently and furiously as a reflection of the mood of the narrative.

Areas of prayer focus around the church:

- Upturned bowls under green fabric will 'landscape' an area. Incorporate a flat shallow dish of water and small pebbles, or sand around a mirror. Have small arrangements of flowers or leaves.
- Use newspaper headlines and pictures among the prayer suggestions.
- Prayer suggestions: 'Pray for all who are worried and anxious'; 'Pray for the grace to trust God better'; 'Pray for our world, thanking God for it'; 'Thank God for the gift of life, and pray for the grace to live it well'.
- Have a globe or picture of the planet.

Sunday before Lent, Years ABC

Focus of the service: Jesus is transfigured, showing the glory of God.
Mood: Awe and wonder. Mystery and holiness.

Possibilities for worship:

- Silver and green streamers and flags for sung times of worship.
- Instruments like bells and triangles and xylophone played gently at the Gloria or Sanctus.
- Lots of candles, perhaps in clusters on window ledges or as part of flower arrangements.
- Lit candles held by children around the altar at the Eucharistic Prayer.
- Attention drawn to any stained glass with the light shining through. If you happen to have a window of the transfiguration, gather round it at the gospel (or turn to face it).
- Moving coloured water projected using OHP (see page 27).
- During the Gospel pause at the moment of transfiguration with music of wonder and mystery while candles are lit. Continue music quietly through until Jesus is left alone with his disciples. Fade music and extinguish candles.
- Project the word 'Life' in plain bubble writing during the time of Penitence and have a corresponding acetate which is decorated with colours and swirls. Place this over the first one as the words of forgiveness are proclaimed.

Areas of prayer focus around the church:

- Green and silver fabric.
- Stones and pebbles with candles among them, on a mirror or foil.
- Pictures from newspapers and magazines – local and international – where God's transforming is needed.
- Prayer suggestions: 'Open our eyes to see your glory'; 'Make our lives shine with your love'; 'Pray for all who are blinded by prejudice, fear or hate'; 'Pray that the Church may be a sign of God's kingdom'; 'Pray for all who are hurting or confused'. Print separately and place among the stones and pictures.

The season of Lent

The English name of this season is linked with the lengthening spring days of the northern hemisphere, and it was originally a time of preparation of those approaching their Easter baptism. There are accordingly strong links with Jesus' preparation for his ministry, a 40-day process of prayer and fasting spent wrestling with how best to proclaim the kingdom.

During the week Ash Wednesday is an occasion of collective sorrow or sin and recognition of God's grace, mercy and forgiveness, so that together as church we can all use this season of penitence creatively. We wrestle with the problem of evil and our fractured relationship with God, tracing the human story through scripture, and always aware of Jesus' power to heal and restore.

Like Advent, the colour of this season is purple, right up to Palm Sunday, because we are exploring the rich but dark areas of our humanity. Many church communities will meet in small groups during the weekdays of Lent to be discipled and to pray. Traditionally the church building is bare of flowers, and fasting from luxuries or addressing a particular weakness is also practised. The mood is of real longing for God's healing and guidance in our lives and in the whole human condition, so it is really all about holiness and humility.

This doesn't mean that Lent is a season of long faces and self-flagellation. There is a wholesome maturity about setting a season for facing these issues, and an excitement about the way God works in us to heal and transform. In our worship we need to provide space and opportunity for people to meet honestly with God and allow the healing and transforming to happen.

Each Sunday in every season also retains the affirming joy of resurrection, of course, and on Mothering Sunday – the fourth in Lent – we celebrate our thankfulness for practical loving care in all relationships, and in particular our human parenting and God's parenting of us. What better seasonal landscape to host such celebration.

By the fifth Sunday of Lent, the shadow of the cross is more sharply defined, and we prepare to get back into 'real time' to walk with Jesus through that last week of his life on earth before crucifixion. This starts with Palm Sunday, and the colour changes from purple to red, the colour of lifeblood and sacrifice. The following week is sometimes known as Holy Week. Instinctively we want our buildings to express this heightened awareness of Christ's saving death, and many churches install a bare wooden cross as a focus for this time. There are no flowers, as if we are fasting. In some churches any statues are covered up from the fifth Sunday onwards, so that nothing distracts from the stark reality of the Passion. It is a week of spiritually journeying together, for Spring Harvest or Iona; for a parish pilgrimage around the church or further afield; for daily gathered prayer, or a community commitment to read a complete gospel during the week.

On Palm Sunday we enact in our worship the procession into Jerusalem, tasting the bittersweet emotions of the crowd's hosannas and their call for Jesus' execution. This was an all-age crowd if ever there was one, with the children's voices recorded as ringing out with a truth the authorities found offensive. If you haven't tried it before, do consider having a procession through the streets today as part of the worship, with waving branches and streamers. Some even have a donkey, though this is not an essential item! Involve different voices in the gospel account of the events.

Passover meals are another way of entering into the whole story as a community, and there are scripts available for this (see Resources, page 115). Often these are held on Maundy Thursday – the day of Jesus' last supper with his disciples, either as an extended Eucharist or as a separate Agape meal. Increasingly churches of all traditions are valuing the idea of a garden set up in the church as a focus for watching and praying on a rota basis during the evening and night of that Thursday.

Good Friday is one of those occasions in the year when there is a real longing for unity, as we share this day together. Think about places in your area where a walk in the way of the cross might involve all local churches, working together on planning each stopping place along the route to reflect on the meaning of the cross. Such walks are whole community events, and wonderful opportunities for God to work on healing our divisions.

First Sunday of Lent, Years ABC

Focus of the service: Temptation. Jesus in the desert.
Mood: Serious and self-aware. Attentive to what God is saying to us.

Possibilities for worship:

- Purple streamers and flags available during singing.
- Bowl of incense or fragrant oil burner burning during time of Penitence.
- In all three years the Old Testament reading can be dramatised or read chorally, with music background.
- Use two different voices for the conversation in the Gospel.
- Project an image of the Judean desert and of large pebbles or boulders as a focus in time of Penitence and Gospel.
- Year B: projected images of water and rainbow.
- Have a 'Hints for dealing with temptation' display during Lent where people of all ages can write (or have scribed) methods they have found useful in the battle of good over evil.

Areas of prayer focus around the church:

- Purple fabric.
- A few large smooth stones and some bread rolls all together.
- Two apples with bites taken out of them.
- Large question marks.
- Soundbites from the Gospel printed out separately among the images and prayer suggestions.
- Prayer suggestions: 'Pray for those battling with temptation at the moment'; 'Pray for all who lead and all who advise – for wisdom and integrity'; 'Pray for our wills to be lined up with God's will'; 'Pray for all who go hungry and thirsty'; 'Pray for those who have more than enough and refuse to share'; 'Pray for those who don't know what to do for the best'.

Second Sunday of Lent, Years ABC

Focus of the service: Living by faith in God.
Mood: Possibly disturbing – shaking us up. An honest look at the implications of the faith life. Challenging.

Possibilities for worship:

- Purple streamers and flags available for times of singing.
- At time of Penitence use some of the ideas from 'Using the senses' (see page 20).
- Use music as a background to the Old Testament reading as God speaks to Abraham.
- Have different voices in the Gospel conversations.
- Projected images of the desert again, of the effects of a strong wind blowing (sailing boats, balloons, flags).
- Give space for people to be in silence waiting on God, using music to help reach the stillness, and a visual focus such as one of the windows, the cross or a projected painting such as Holman Hunt's 'The Light of the World'.

Areas of prayer focus around the church:

- Purple fabric or sand and rock arranged on plastic sheeting.
- Candles available to light.
- Pictures of contrasts in lifestyle and facilities available worldwide.
- Print out soundbites from the readings and place them among the pictures.
- Suggestions for prayer: 'Pray that we may wake up to what it means to live by faith in God'; 'Pray for those who find it very hard to trust God'; 'Pray for the grace to follow wherever God leads us'; 'Pray that we may not get in God's way or make it difficult for others to know him'.

Third Sunday of Lent, Years ABC

Focus of the service: God's lavish and generous invitation to us, and the cost of responding with love and obedience.
Mood: Freeing, healing and also challenging.

Possibilities for worship:
- Green and blue streamers like water, or purple for the continuing Lenten colour.
- Recorded sounds of running water during the 'thirsty' Old Testament reading (Years A and C).
- Year A: have the Gospel read in parts from a dramatised Bible (or DIY).
- Year B: act out the Gospel.
- Projected images of water, and an ancient pathway or stone stairway.
- If the church has the Ten Commandments written up, focus on them during the time of Penitence, or use symbols for each of the commandments.
- Choose soundbites and write them large in bubble writing on lining paper with crayons available for colouring.
- Have the font open and full, with a towel so people can use it. Place the words 'Living God, satisfy our thirst' placed beside it.

Areas of prayer focus around the church:
- Use the font as one of the focus areas for prayer.
- Purple fabric, or sand and stones with water.
- Have a jug of water and bowl.
- Pictures and information of fresh water projects worldwide.
- A Bible open at the readings for today.
- Prayer suggestions: 'Pray for all who thirst for meaning in their lives'; 'Pray for those who have been baptised in this church'; 'Pray for courage to stand firm when the life of faith is challenging'; 'Pray for greater generosity of spirit'.

Fourth Sunday of Lent (Mothering Sunday), Years ABC

Focus of the service: Thanksgiving for earthly mothering of all kinds. Thanks for God's parenting of us.
Mood: Thankfulness and appreciation. Loving care and affirmation. Festive. Refreshing.

Possibilities for worship:

- Pink and purple streamers, strips of cloth hangings, banners or flags.
- Bells and shakers.
- Projected images of mothering – people, animals and birds, spring beauty in nature.
- Lots of flowers, both in arrangements and in small posies for giving to one another.
- Act out the Old Testament reading with music background.
- Short interview with different generations of mums and different generations of children.
- A 'God's parenting' display on stands or projected: 'God is . . .'
- If using the second Gospel choice, focus on any places in the building which show Mary and John at the cross.
- Sounds of birdsong as people come in and during Communion.

Areas of prayer focus around the church:

- Pink and purple fabric with flowers among stones and 'mother and child' images from nature.
- Candles and quiet, refreshing music.
- One prayer focus for candles and flowers in memory of mothers who have died.
- Use the decorated font for a prayer focus of healing of damaged relationships.
- Prayer suggestions: 'Thank God for all good mothering and all loving, caring relationships'; 'Pray for all families'; 'Give thanks for God's forgiveness and loving kindness'; 'Help us understand one another's needs better'; 'We are all your children – help us grow in love'.

Fifth Sunday of Lent, Years ABC

Focus of the service: The way Jesus can transform suffering and death into life and hope.

Mood: Solemn. An engagement with the deep questions about life and death. Hope in the heart of suffering.

Possibilities for worship:

- Purple and hessian or unbleached cotton.
- Recorded music with an ache in it – such as *Schindler's List* or *Gladiator* – as a background to the Old Testament reading.
- Ongoing painting by one praying person during the worship, on a large scale (sheeting or lining paper), of the cross with a sense of glory as well as darkness.
- Projected images of dark thunderclouds with brightness, and of the bright day from inside the dark walls of a cave.
- Oil burner or bowl of incense during the Gospel.
- Shakers and wood blocks, etc., accompanying Ezekiel's dry bones vision.
- At the time of Penitence use Allegri's *Miserere* with the words 'Have mercy on me, O God' projected as they are carefully written.
- For the Creed say the 'Glory to the Father, and to the Son . . .' and ask everyone to pause, catching their breath, immediately after 'is now . . .'

Areas of prayer focus around the church:

- Have water available at the font with a towel, and images of the washing of feet.
- Use the whole building, drawing people to focus on any windows or architecture as symbols to direct their prayer. (There is often a variety of ways the Passion is portrayed.)
- Purple fabric, rocks, thorns, a cross.
- Prayer suggestions: 'Pray for those who are grieving'; 'Pray for a deeper awareness of living eternal life here and now'; 'Pray for courage for those going through times of darkness and shadow'; 'Pray for a clearer and more honest understanding of who we are'; 'Pray for a cleansing of all motives'.
- Have headlines and news pictures placed among the prayer intentions with sticky notes and pens available to write prayers on.

Palm Sunday, Years ABC

Focus of the service: Jesus entering Jerusalem on a donkey. The Servant King facing rejection and death to free us from everlasting death.

Mood: Bitter/sweet. Rejoicing and yet heavy with the shadow of the cross. Fresh awareness of our own human fickleness.

Possibilities for worship:

- Purple hangings. Plain cross draped with cloth, the base in among stones.
- Symbols of Jesus' death brought to the cross during the offertory – nails, hammer, dice, rope, coins thrown down from a bag, thorns, a tall reed.
- Palm branches, any branches, streamers and flags for the procession, preferably outside. Songs that everyone can sing at a pitch they can reach, during the procession. Even a donkey, perhaps.
- Dramatised choral reading of the long Gospel, involving the whole gathered people. Or try a recorded version.
- Where there are Stations of the Cross, walk in procession around these as the story is narrated. Or make a 'Way of the Cross' outside and all around the church with the Gospel read as everyone walks it together.
- At some point in the worship, encourage everyone who can, to kneel, even if this isn't usual practice.
- For the time of Penitence, place a cross on the floor of lit candles in sand.
- Projected images of the Crucifixion through art.

Areas of prayer focus around the church:

- Stones, thorns, with soundbites from the Gospel narrative printed among them.
- Focus on the crosses around the building.
- Provide tiny crosses to hold and place in the prayer areas.
- Different images of Christ projected or displayed
- Prayer suggestions: 'Pray for the world to want God's kingdom'; 'Pray for God's peace which the world cannot give'; 'Pray for those imprisoned who are innocent'; 'Pray for better discernment to recognise propaganda for what it is and hold firm to truth'.

Holy Week

Maundy Thursday, Years ABC

Focus of the service: The Last Supper. The Passover with new meaning of Bread and Wine. Servanthood and foot-washing. The command to love one another as Jesus loves us.

Mood: Solemn and important for the whole community. Reflective and thankful. Mystical.

Possibilities for worship:

- Consider a Eucharist in the context of a Passover meal (see page 115).
- White and gold cloth, streamers and flags.
- Projected images of foot-washing, bread and wine, wheat and grapes.
- Bread and wine with wheat and grapes in a focal display.
- Foot-washing – with several bowls and towels so everyone can wash one another's feet.
- A 'Garden of Gethsemane' vigil of prayer during the night.

Good Friday, Years ABC

Focus of the service: The Crucifixion. Jesus loving us even to death. Love that saves us and sets us free.

Mood: Solemn. Sad. Penitential. Thankful. Touching the raw places of our deepest reality. Love for Jesus.

Possibilities for worship:

- Have the church building open for prayer, with focuses that introduce people to Jesus and the extent of God's forgiving love for us all.
- Join with Christians from other churches for a combined walk and service using readings from the Gospel, prayers and music.
- Collect a whole range of images of the Crucifixion and of Christ from art, and encourage people to wander around them, choosing one that draws them, while music is playing.
- Make a prayer trail of the Way of the Cross around the church grounds or a local beauty spot, and have copies like a nature trail so visitors can follow it on their own or in small groups.

The season of Easter

Celebrating Easter after the whole church community has reflected together so deeply on the events leading to Jesus' crucifixion is a life-changing experience, and one which sends echoes through the rest of the year, and through our very identity as Easter People. It is so much more than a decorated church full of spring flowers, lovely as this is. There is no reason why the whole community shouldn't share in an Easter Vigil service, either on the Saturday evening or before dawn on the Sunday, taking part actively in the unfolding of the story and becoming part of that story in the process.

Gathering in the darkness round a bonfire marks the night as special and frees up our imaginations to wonder as we marvel at the mysterious truth of resurrection. For me, worshipping as dawn breaks is about the most powerful context for remembering Jesus bursting out of death into new life. From the baby candle flames flickering at midnight as we recalled the birth of Christ to the full-blown blaze of the sun's rising at Easter is fire at its most sacramental. And following this with shared breakfast, Easter egg hunting and a day of celebration somehow fastens the whole of our life experience in a New Life focus.

Still in 'real time', the season of Easter continues full of celebration and wonder, the colour gold or white right up to the Ascension and on into that expectant nine days, marking the apostles' prayerful wait for the gift Jesus had promised. Then, with the noise and force of a strong wind blowing, and looking something like flame, the Holy Spirit of God breathes right into those attentive and expectant disciples, baptising them into a whole new way of earthly life, lived in the dimension of eternal life.

Pentecost was already the Jewish festival of the early harvest; what was this outpouring if not a lavish and abundant fulfilment of such a festival? Perhaps we should have another fire to celebrate Pentecost, and a first-fruits harvest to remind us of the fruit of Spirit-filled lives.

The colour is either white, or red, the colour of fire.

Easter Eve, Years ABC

Focus of the service: The waiting and hoping of the people of God. The excitement of new life, of light in the darkness, of the resurrection.

Mood: Expectant. Hopeful. Receptive. A strong awareness of being bound together as God's people.

Possibilities for worship:

- Meet when it is dark, either on the Saturday evening or very early on Easter morning. Gather round a bonfire, either at the church or somewhere like the beach or on a hill.

- If the bonfire is some distance from the church, either have the whole service there or have a night hike back to the church after the stories, with soup at the church when you arrive. Or have stories on the way as you walk with a flaming torch (or protected candles) lit from the fire.

- Tell the stories of the Great Story in a variety of ways – acting, storytelling, in conversation, with music, with images projected, with sound effects, involving everyone.

- Candlelight – with the candles all lit from the one candle.

- Bells brought from home and rung in a burst of praise at the Gloria. Party poppers. Balloons. Kites.

Easter Day, Years ABC

> **Focus of the service:** Resurrection. Jesus, risen from death and alive for ever. Victory of love and life over sin and death.
> **Mood:** Joy. Celebration. Praise. Excitement. Thankfulness. Wonder.

Possibilities for worship:

- White, silver and gold streamers, coloured banners and flags.
- Large paper butterflies to colour and fix on sticks.
- Bells, chime bars, shakers, party poppers, especially at the Gloria and in the festive hymns.
- An Easter garden, or many, with the empty tomb and the empty crosses.
- The plain wooden cross of Good Friday decorated with flowers.
- The service early in the morning, followed by breakfast and Easter egg hunt.
- A basket of ordinary eggs as a sign of new life.
- Projected pictures of sunrise, eggs and chicks, the 'garden tomb' or stone crosses with the sun shining behind them.

Areas of prayer focus around the church:

- Wrap wire mesh around a rough cross made from the trunk of last year's Christmas tree and invite people to push flowers into the mesh as they pray.
- Use the Easter garden as one of the focuses for prayer.
- White and gold fabric, and candles on a mirror or in water.
- Soundbites from the Gospel printed out and placed among pictures of areas of the world's darkness and pain.
- Suggestions for prayer, to be printed separately and placed in each area: 'Pray for the world to know God's saving love'; 'Pray that the church may live out her hope in love and joy'; 'Give thanks to God for this victory of good over evil and life over death'; 'Jesus is alive – talk to him now. Tell him the things that weigh on your heart.'

Second Sunday of Easter, Years ABC

Focus of the service: Knowing that Jesus is alive changes the way people live.
Mood: Celebration and joy. Amazement and hope.

Possibilities for worship:

- Streamers, banners and flags of white, gold and silver.
- Instruments available to play during suitable hymns and the Gloria.
- Recorded music of festive celebration as people come in.
- Project an image of God's glory in the natural world, and overlay it with statements about God's loving kindness and faithfulness. Everyone reads them aloud in any order, so there is a sound of many voices proclaiming their praise.
- Images of starburst, dawn, fireworks, or silhouette shadows of the empty tomb.
- Dramatise the Gospel, either miming while it is read, or use an OHP with shadow puppets. Use music or sounds to create mood.

Areas of prayer focus around the church:

- Floating candles in water.
- Gold or brocade fabric (curtains) with strips of white cotton.
- The Easter gardens and the cross.
- Soundbites printed out and placed among pictures and headlines of concern – such as 'My Lord and my God!' or 'Peace be with you'.
- Prayer suggestions: 'Jesus is alive. Jesus is here with us now . . .'; 'Pray for any who are anxious or timid'; 'Pray for anyone blinded by wealth or poverty'; 'Pray for those unable to get to church today'; 'The Lord is my light and my salvation'.

Third Sunday of Easter, Years ABC

Focus of the service: The risen Jesus recognised in the breaking of bread.
Mood: Inspiring and affirming in our Christian hope. Joyful.

Possibilities for worship:

- Streamers, flags and banners of white, gold and all colours.
- Candles lit and held during the Eucharistic Prayer, as the bread is blessed and broken.
- Recorded music background to the Gospel – before the reading, at natural spaces for taking in what is being said, and continuing after the reading has finished.
- In the readings from Acts, involve the whole congregation in the words of the crowds. Have the words displayed, projected or printed on the weekly handout.
- On a length of lining paper draw in the branches and twigs of a tree. Have available cut-out green tissue paper leaves and glue for children to stick on the foliage.
- Project images of bread, wheat, light and shadow.
- Year C: have the sound effects of ocean surf during the Gospel.

Areas of prayer focus around the church:

- Use the Easter garden, the font, and any relevant stained glass windows as focuses for prayer.
- Print out soundbites from the readings (such as 'Didn't our hearts burn within us . . . ?') and place these in the prayer areas.
- Prayer suggestions: 'Pray for those who have yet to discover that Jesus is alive'; 'Pray for everyone who is feeling very sad and disappointed'; 'Pray that we may recognise Jesus'; 'Pray that as we read the Bible we may be shown its meaning'; 'Pray for the grace to be hospitable and welcoming to strangers'.

Fourth Sunday of Easter, Years ABC

Focus of the service: Jesus is the Good Shepherd. (The shepherd passage is spread over the three years.) The Power of Jesus.
Mood: Celebration at the liberating nature of resurrection. Exploration of what it means for us.

Possibilities for worship:

- Yellow, gold and white streamers and banners.
- Large pictures of sheep and shepherd being painted or collaged during Psalm 23.
- Recorded sounds of bleating sheep and birdsong during the Gospel.
- Year C: read the Revelation passage chorally, using the whole congregation.
- Words of Psalm 23 written out for colouring and decorating.
- Cut-outs of sheep given out as a physical focus for the time of Penitence.

Areas of prayer focus around the church:

- Upturned bowls draped with green cloth, with a blue scarf 'stream' flowing through the hills
- Have the words of Psalm 23 printed out either as a unit, or separately in different sections
- Prayer suggestions: 'Pray for a fresh awareness of the risen Jesus'; 'Pray for one another'; 'Pray for all church communities'; 'Long for people to hear God's love and respond to it'.
- Cut-outs of sheep for people to write prayers or prayer concerns on and place on the hilly landscape.

Fifth Sunday of Easter, Years ABC

Focus of the service: Living with Jesus – the new 'Way' to live.
Mood: Bound together in God's love. Celebrating fresh understanding of the risen life. Excited by this new relationship with Jesus.

Possibilities for worship:
- Gold, white and silver streamers, banners and flags.
- Instruments and dancing (as worship, not performance) during the Gloria and some of the hymns.
- Year A: give out stones for people to hold as they bring to God the times when they know they are stone-hearted. As the stone warms up in their hand, remind them of God's forgiving love warming our hearts to make us more loving.
- Year B: decorate the church with vines cut from green paper and clusters of grapes from purple paper.
- Have everyone holding hands, making a 'vine' which stretches over the whole church, at the exchange of the Peace.
- Projected images of a pathway or road, or of grapes on a vine, or a stone built wall.
- For the Creed, sing the hymn 'I believe in Jesus'.

Areas of prayer focus around the church:
- Gold and white fabric.
- Grapes/stones.
- Pictures of relationships from all different cultures and age groups.
- Soundbites from the Gospel printed out and placed among the pictures and candles.
- Prayer suggestions: 'Pray for those we love and care for'; 'Pray for broken friendships and fractured families'; 'Welcome God into all your conversations and meetings this week'; 'Ask God to develop your relationship with him'; 'Pray for all who feel cut off from God'.

Sixth Sunday of Easter, Years ABC

Focus of the service: Jesus prepares his friends for leaving them without his physical presence. The Way of Love.
Mood: Encouraging and affirming. Reflective. Celebrating Jesus being alive for ever.

Possibilities for worship:

- Gold, white and coloured streamers and flags.
- Bells, chimes, rainsticks.
- Recorded sounds of jazz, folk or chamber music, where the woven strands of melody can be heard, as a sound picture of a loving community.
- Give people a heart-shaped piece of paper to hold and focus on during the time of Penitence.
- Projected images of Jesus healing, talking with his disciples and so on, taken from paintings or using paper silhouettes (see 'Using an OHP creatively', page 27).
- Soundbites from the readings printed in bubble writing for colouring, either individually sized or communally sized on flipchart paper or lining paper.
- Write on the centre of an acetate 'Our God is . . .' and collect everyone's ideas about what God is like, recording them around the central statement. Then everyone reads their way through all the statements, in any order, so there is a quiet buzz of people proclaiming God all over the church. As the last voices finish speaking, gather up all the reflective celebration by saying, 'Our God IS. Amen.'

Areas of prayer focus around the church:

- Gold and white fabric.
- Grouped candles in bowls.
- Pictures of people living as God's friends – caring for one another and supporting one another.
- Prayer suggestions: 'Pray for people to love and respect one another'; 'Pray for peace and justice, and for everyone who is oppressed'; 'Pray for all in positions of responsibility and authority'; 'Thank God for being with us every moment in every situation'.

Ascension Day, Years ABC

Focus of the service: Jesus returning to heaven not through death but life. Giving Jesus thanks, honour and worship as Lord.
Mood: A sense of completion and accomplishment, victory and fulfilment.

Possibilities for worship:
- Silver, blue and white streamers and flags.
- Projected images of starbirth, a blaze of light, fireworks or dramatic skyscape. Paintings of the Ascension from a variety of artists and cultures.
- Recorded music to accompany the narrative of the Ascension, using it to set the mood first and then give room for reflection during the reading.
- Let off a helium balloon with an Ascension message.

Areas of prayer focus around the church:
- Silver, white and blue fabric.
- Candles.
- Cut-out clouds of white paper for writing prayer requests and placing on the fabric among the candles.
- Prayer suggestions: 'Pray for the worldwide Church'; 'Thank God for those who have kept the message alive'; 'Thank God for those who have helped you get to know Jesus'; 'Pray for the grace to pass the message on effectively'.

Seventh Sunday of Easter, Years ABC

Focus of the service: Living the new resurrection life in the real world of suffering and temptation.
Mood: Expectant. Looking forward to the gift of God's Holy Spirit. A sense of the worldly values turned on their head.

Possibilities for worship:

- Provide space for expectant waiting on God, using 'wide landscape' music to settle people and open up their listening.
- Projected images of still, quiet land- and seascapes with natural sounds.
- Encourage people to stand, sit or kneel all around the church building, waiting in stillness.
- Have people of all ages holding lit candles around the sanctuary at the Eucharistic Prayer.
- Use a music background to the Gospel reading.
- Dramatise the reading from Acts.
- Have projected images of glory in nature, overlaid with a cut-out cross (or have an actual cross placed on the acetate so that the silhouette shows on the screen or wall).

Areas of prayer focus around the church:

- Blue fabric with white paper or cloth cut-out clouds, or white and gold fabric.
- Print out soundbites from the day's Gospel and place among images of the glory of nature and newspaper headlines.
- Prayer suggestions: 'Pray that we may be true to our calling in this place'; 'Pray for the other groups of Christians locally'; 'Pray for those with difficult decisions and choices to make'; 'Help us make all our choices in your company'.

Pentecost, Years ABC

Focus of the service: The Holy Spirit of God is poured out on the expectant disciples.
Mood: Celebration and re-membering, or reliving of the event. Expectant. New confidence.

Possibilities for worship:
- Red, orange and yellow (flame-coloured) streamers, banners and flags.
- Have three flame-coloured flags pointing in to a central focus, being lifted and lowered as they are waved.
- Recorded sound of a strong wind, or fans, or streamers, as the Acts passage is read.
- Projected images of fire, or swirling colour, or water.
- Different interpretations of the event in art.
- Extend the Eucharist to incorporate a parish shared meal or picnic.
- Give everyone a cut-out flame to focus on during the time of Penitence and the sermon. Exchange these with other people at the Peace.
- Have the good news (John 3:16, for instance) proclaimed in different languages.
- Encourage everyone to pray the Lord's Prayer together but in their mother tongue, or in the English version they find most natural.

Areas of prayer focus around the church:
- Orange, red and yellow fabric and small flower arrangements of white and red.
- Candles on mirrors or in water.
- Pictures of people from all over the world and through the ages and traditions.
- Prayer suggestions: 'Pray that we may be set on fire with love for God'; 'Pray for the Church to witness faithfully in today's world and in ways that touch hearts'; 'Pray for those who preach and teach'.

The season of Ordinary Time

There has been a great sweep of sustained 'real time' focus, as the whole Church throughout the world walks the Way of the Cross, out into the light of the Resurrection and on to the outpouring of God's Spirit on his people. In our human makeup there is now a need for a quieter time of growth and assimilation, and opportunity to explore the treasures of Jesus' identity and his earthly ministry, and to mull over the extraordinary events of Easter and Pentecost.

For this we resume the season of Ordinary Time, and the growth colour of green, marking the entrance to it with the festival of Trinity. (The idea of festival wins out here over the growth colour, so that Trinity Sunday itself is festive white.) Since all of this time is helping us deepen our understanding of God's nature, the Sundays from June right around to October are all named Sundays after Trinity, and give the Church space to meditate on the one true God who is Father, Son and Spirit.

These Sundays allow us to settle into the tone and style of a particular Gospel each year, so there is room for theological debate in focused Bible studies. Often Lent and Advent are taken as being the times for particular courses of study, but I wonder if this time of Trinity is an excellent time to encourage shared reading and praying around the Gospel of the year, either in groups or individually during the week, so that on Sunday the gathered community have shared their preparation of the set readings, led by a short commentary given out on the previous Sunday or published in the newsletter.

Northern hemisphere churches are following the Sundays after Trinity through the summer, with opportunities for church walks and picnics included in an extended Eucharist from time to time, community shared meals, parties or dances, and the possibility of a church holiday, either self-planned or linking up with Greenbelt, World Village, Taizé or New Wine. With separate children's provision often stopping for the sake of the leaders during the school holidays, the quieter Sundays of August can become times to try more of the whole community worship.

As the season of Ordinary Time reflection progresses, it begins looking forward to focus on the reign of Christ in earth and heaven, coinciding with the festival of All Saints' Day at the beginning of November, and the November commemorations of our departed loved ones, Remembrance Day and Christ as King. With the shift in focus can come a shift in colour, from green to red, like the poppies we wear at this time of year. Instead of taking their name from Trinity, these Sundays are a countdown to Advent, sometimes known as the kingdom season, so that the year comes full circle, bringing us to a point where we are ready to engage with those Last Things and the big questions of life and death in preparation for the festival of Christmas, following a slightly different emphasis now, because of the change of Gospel.

Trinity Sunday, Years ABC

Focus of the service: The threefold nature of the One God.
Mood: Celebration. Wonder. Thankfulness. Mystery.

Possibilities for worship:
- Streamers and flags for worship, in different colours of green, and silver or white.
- Triangles and bells to play during the singing.
- A large Celtic knotwork pattern of the Trinity in string, taped to the floor so young children can walk along the lines of it.
- Gather around the font for the time of confession and forgiveness and splash water around as a sign of God's cleansing forgiveness.
- Projected images of Celtic knotwork, where a pattern of 'threeness' is actually one unbroken line.
- Images of nature expressing God's nature – like sea and sky, sun, moon and stars, weather and growth.
- Prepare and make copies of the Old Testament reading to be read communally, some verses by men and boys, some by women and girls and some by everyone.
- If you have a band or music group, have three instruments playing together in harmony as people think about the character of God.

Areas of prayer focus around the church:
- Green and silver fabric.
- Flower arrangement with just three stems.
- Copies of the Celtic patterns.
- Pictures of current local, national and international concerns.
- Prayer suggestions printed out separately and placed among the pictures: 'For those who suffer in body, mind or spirit'; 'For those who are haunted by the past or fearful of the future'; 'For a deeper understanding of who God is and what God is like'; 'For God to make us more loving and forgiving'; 'For all who do not know that God loves them'.

Sundays after Trinity: Proper 4, Years ABC

(Sunday between 29 May and 4 June)

Year A: Wise to act on God's Word
Year B: Authority over the Sabbath
Year C: God's authority to heal

Focus of the service: God's Law filled again with God's life. Jesus showing us what God's authority is like. Putting faith into action.
Mood: Challenging. Rallying. Reassuring.

Possibilities for worship:

- Act out the Gospel for each year. In Year A people form the buildings and the stormy rivers.
- Make the Creed an invitation to 'walk the talk', perhaps saying the words with one hand raised.
- If appropriate and practical, make a large ring of people in pairs around the church. As everyone chants, 'Walk the talk' they walk through a grand chain (passing everyone by holding hands, alternate right and left).
- Images of God's authority, shown in works of art, and in grand, dramatic scenery.
- Green streamers and flags.
- Recorded music which resonates with the quiet, firm and loving authority of God – such as Pachelbel's Canon, Tallis, Handel or Bach.
- Building bricks and construction toys to play with, on either a firm or wobbly surface.

Areas of prayer focus around the church:

- Green fabric.
- Headlines and images of topical prayer concerns from newspapers and magazines.
- Particular prayer needs printed out separately and placed among the pictures: 'Pray that people may hear the whisper of God and act on it'; 'Pray for those who find it hard to trust God's love and forgiveness'; 'Pray for a purifying of our motives, so we are increasingly at one with ourselves and with God'; 'Pray for God to help us get our priorities right'.

Sundays after Trinity: Proper 5, Years ABC

(Sunday between 5 and 11 June)

Year A: Bringing dead lives to life
Year B: Evil is driven out by goodness
Year C: Restoring the dead to life

Focus of the service: God's power to transform and renew, to heal even the dead. Can we accept Jesus' power and love or do we distrust it?
Mood: Challenge. Who is this Jesus? Hope in the darkest places.

Possibilities for worship:

- As people come in, have a basket of folded papers (like a raffle). Label the basket 'Life in all its fullness on offer – for those who pick a winning ticket'. Every piece of folded paper has on it 'YES, YOU!' Everyone holds their winning tickets at the time of Confession and as they hear God's words of forgiveness spoken to them.

- Green flags, banners and streamers – all shades, from very dark to sparkling.

- Projected images of 'new life' in plants, animals and people; gravestones with flowers and sunlight; sunrise.

- Recorded music with a sense of hope and new life beginning, such as 'Morning' from Grieg's *Peer Gynt Suite*, Vaughan Williams' *Variations on 'Greensleeves'*, or the 'Thanksgiving after the storm' from Beethoven's *Pastoral Symphony*.

- A recording of a heartbeat during the Gospel reading in Years A and C.

- The Gospel can be mimed during the telling – in Years A and C use the aisle as the street and invite everyone out into it so the action takes place in the middle of the church. In Year B do stylised, symbolic actions.

Areas of prayer focus around the church:

- Dark and light green cloth. Lamplight or candlelight.

- Pictures which speak about deep needs in life-threatening situations, such as drought, famine, natural disasters or war-related deprivation.

- Among the pictures have 'Lord, hear our prayer', written on a rainbow.

- Have the words of today's Collect written out carefully in the centre of each prayer area, together with soundbites from the day's readings.
- Have cards for signing for anyone unwell, or going through an especially dark patch at the moment.
- Let people light candles for their own loved ones, and have sticky notes available for names and prayers.

Sundays after Trinity: Proper 6, Years ABC

(Sunday between 12 and 18 June)

Year A: Announcing the kingdom with signs
Year B: How the kingdom grows
Year C: Signs of love and forgiveness

> **Focus of the service:** Jesus teaching about the kingdom of God. Us being signs of the kingdom.
> **Mood:** Challenging for our commitment to discipleship. Attentiveness to Jesus. Reading the signs to understand spiritual things.

Possibilities for worship:

- Around the church or on a handout have 'What is God like?' clues – such as pictures of a night sky, planet Earth, a baby being cuddled, animals feeding, and a candle burning. After the Gospel people look at the pictures with the question in mind and talk about their ideas.
- Green streamers and flags; leafy branches for waving.
- Verses or phrases from today's readings in bubble writing to colour in, or a larger version for people to decorate with leaves and petals.
- For Year A have the sounds of footsteps during the Gospel, for Year B have birdsong, and for Year C have perfume in the air during the Gospel reading.
- Have flags with the qualities of the kingdom of God written on them: Love; Forgiveness; Freedom; Peace; Healing; Joy. Wave these flags during the Gloria, at the Sanctus and in one or two hymns.

Areas of prayer focus around the church:

- Use green fabric.
- Make tiny flower arrangements in plastic lids filled with oasis and place several of them on each prayer area.
- Make one area a display of someone the church supports in mission, with prayer concerns and needs.
- Have an open letter for people to write in their prayers.

Sundays after Trinity: Proper 7, Years ABC

(Sunday between 19 and 25 June)

Focus of the service: Jesus speaks into our fear and his presence brings us peace.
Mood: Reassuring. Comforting.

Possibilities for worship:

- Images of peace and tranquillity displayed or projected.
- The words 'Don't be afraid – I am here' written huge and displayed on the walls.
- Soundbites in bubble writing to be coloured in and decorated: Year A – Matthew 10:30; Year B – Mark 4:40; and Year C – Luke 8:35: 'They found the man . . . sitting at the feet of Jesus, clothed and in his right mind.'
- During the Gospel for Year B have the sounds of the sea. Or while it is read have a large sheet or small parachute held by a group of people and moved gently and vigorously expressing the narrative.
- Use different voices for the Gospel in Year C, and background music of something quiet but with a sense of urgency and approaching danger in it. Either an appropriate film soundtrack or music by Mahler or Sibelius, perhaps.
- During a reflective, quiet song, use a rainstick or soft bells.
- Encourage everyone to be completely still and peaceful in the presence of God for about a minute, choosing a place in the church to spend this time of complete stillness.

Areas of prayer focus around the church:

- Use green fabric, and create a display of peace and tranquillity – perhaps with water and stones, and a candle, or one of those indoor miniature fountains.
- Prayer suggestions: 'Speak your peace into our deepest fears, O God'; 'Be still and know that I am God'; 'Pray for anyone who is terrified at the moment. Pray God's peace and confidence into that situation'; 'Pray for those who are growing up in an atmosphere of fear and conflict'; 'Pray for all whose fears, real or imagined, imprison them'; 'Pray for all who are scared to be themselves in case they are rejected'.

Sundays after Trinity: Proper 8, Years ABC

(Sunday between 26 June and 2 July)

Year A: Even a cup of water in my name . . .
Year B: Jairus' daughter restored to life
Year C: The cost of following Jesus

Focus of the service: How we respond to God affects our response to others.
Mood: Challenging. Thought-provoking. Inspiring.

Possibilities for worship:

- Green or multicoloured streamers and flags for worship, and instruments available.
- Time of confession: give everyone a fruit of some kind – a cherry, a grape, or a strawberry. As they hold it, remind everyone that a good plant naturally produces good fruit. In quietness ask God to heal and forgive those things in us that stop us fruiting – hard-heartedness; determination to go our own way; clutter of too much having, wanting or doing; sulking over what went wrong or what we can't have; careful upkeep of our image. As everyone eats their fruit, long for God to heal and forgive, setting us free to fruit naturally, so that others are blessed through the loving way we live.
- Year A: the Hokey Cokey dance can be adapted so that the chorus goes like this – 'Use your life for loving, loving and for caring, use your life for loving; love one another and love your God!' Invite people either to dance in the aisles, or to stay in their places, raising their hands up then down during the chorus.
- Year B: have the gospel acted out, either mimed or with the different parts being spoken. The whole congregation could be making the wailing and crying and Jesus has to shout to tell them to stop. Then everyone laughs – perhaps some are angry. When the girl runs out of the house, everyone can applaud and cheer.
- Year C: have the Gospel read as the reader walks around the church, with a group of disciples, including James and John. As they walk, everyone in the congregation turns to face them all the way round. Different people come out of the places to speak their parts as the reader gets near them.
- Have key phrases from the readings written out large, with colouring crayons available.

- Project images of paths in difficult terrain, mountain climbers in steep places and flowers growing in rocky ground.
- Use music as a background to the time of confession.

Areas of prayer focus around the church:

- Draw attention to any appropriate pictures in the windows, and use pictures from art which link with the readings.
- Prayer suggestions: 'Pray that God's love will spill out into our attitudes and behaviour with other people'; 'Pray for those finding their walk with God difficult or dangerous'; 'Pray for those we will have the privilege to meet and serve this week'; 'Pray for those we will have the privilege of forgiving this week'; 'Pray for all those whose loved ones are ill, and those who are grieving'.

Sundays after Trinity: Proper 9, Years ABC

(Sunday between 3 and 9 July)

Year A: I will refresh you!
Year B: Closed hearts make us deaf to good news
Year C: God makes us fresh and new

Focus of the service: The life-giving and restoring good news of God's love.
Mood: Liberating, reassuring and thankful.

Possibilities for worship:

- Balloons and multicoloured streamers and flags. Seaside 'windmills' for the little children. Percussion instruments.
- Projected images of refreshing streams and waterfalls, and children splashing around in the water (perhaps people from the church community).
- Chains – made of paper – to use during the confession. At the words of forgiveness the children break them up and throw them in the air, and everyone cheers and claps.
- Have a couple of huge areas of lining paper with paints and sponges, labelled with Matthew 11:28 (Year A), Mark 6:13 (Year B), Luke 10:17 (Year C). Artists express these verses in shape and colour during the first part of the service.
- Base the talk on making a rocket which really fires. Decorate a film canister to look like a rocket with the words 'God's love sets you free!' on it. Half fill the canister with warm water, add two teaspoons of baking powder. Very quickly put on the lid, shake well and stand lid downwards in a safe place on a tray. It will shoot off. When we are fired up with God's love we can shoot off and spread the good news to others.

Areas of prayer focus around the church:

- Green fabric and tiny arrangements of flowers in lids, with candles around them.
- Images of people of all kinds with needs and headlines about troubled areas.
- Prayer suggestions: 'Pray for God's kingdom of love and peace and joy to fill our world'; 'Pray for people to hear what God is saying to us'; 'Pray for those who are sad and hurting'; 'Pray for those who are bringing hope and healing to others'; 'Pray for those who have been put off God by bad experiences of Christians'.

Sundays after Trinity: Proper 10, Years ABC

(Sunday between 10 and 16 July)

Year A: Threats to the growth of God-seed
Year B: Living God's way is dangerous
Year C: God's love meets opposition

Focus of the service: Facing up to the dangers and difficulties of living God's way.
Mood: Candid and challenging. Thankful for God's faithfulness and love.

Possibilities for worship:

- Have open letters and cards for people to write messages of encouragement and support to those who are in prison for being Christian. Names and addresses may be obtained from Amnesty International.
- Just before the declaration of the Creed, light candles and place them on a world map, so that we declare our faith standing alongside those whose lives are endangered or restricted for living that faith out.
- Project images of hands holding a flower, or guarding a flame; images of God's protection and love.
- Have everyone following the cross held high during the last hymn, out into the open, where the blessing is given.
- Give everyone a seed of wheat or barley to hold, and lead people to remember the way God holds us safe in the palm of his hand through all dangers and difficulties. We need to help the God-seed grow in one another.

Areas of prayer focus around the church:

- Have a candle with barbed wire around it.
- Place around the candle the pictures or names and headlines of those places where people are facing persecution at the moment.
- At each prayer focus have the words 'Fear not, little flock. It is the Father's good pleasure to give you the kingdom.'
- Prayer suggestions: 'Pray for those who suffer teasing and persecution for their faith'; 'Pray for the courage to speak out against evil'; 'Thank God for his faithfulness'.

Sundays after Trinity: Proper 11, Years ABC

(Sunday between 17 and 23 July)

Year A: God's mercy and patience in saving us
Year B: Jesus responds to our needs
Year C: Christ has reconciled us to God

Focus of the service: Through Jesus, our loving God reaches out and saves us.
Mood: Good news. Relief and hope, wherever we find ourselves.

Possibilities for worship:

- Different tones of green, and silver streamers and flags for waving during the Gloria and songs of praise.

- Projected images of wheat and weeds (Year A), hands reaching out (Year B), and a bridge (Year C).

- As people take one another's hands at the sharing of the Peace, invite them to feel both God's reaching out and also the sense of being reached out to. Say to one another, 'May God's peace be with you.'

- Use one of the flower arrangements to express the weeds and wheat growing together, Jesus bringing peace and healing into places of dryness and need, or the bridge of reconciliation. Label all of them: 'For God so loved the world . . .'

- Involve different voices in the reading of the Gospel (Year A and Year C) and in the Old Testament reading (Year B).

Areas of prayer focus around the church:

- Have one area where people can pray as they patiently create something beautiful (tiny flower arrangements in milk carton lids). Provide a draped setting with candles for the finished posies.

- Have one area where people pray for others through meditating on God's loving attention to detail and leaving the situations in God's capable hands. (Have an assortment of small natural works of art to be held and wondered at – for example, shells, single flowers, feathers and separate leaves together with prayer concerns in pictures or headlines on cards laid on fabric.)

- Have one area where people pray in small groups about issues brought to mind by the readings. Have the readings displayed, with symbols, and related headings, such as 'The Church', 'The World', 'Our Community', 'Those in need', 'Those who have died and those who mourn'.

Sundays after Trinity: Proper 12, Years ABC

(Sunday between 24 and 30 July)

Year A: How the kingdom grows
Year B: How Jesus feeds us what we need
Year C: To receive we need to ask

Focus of the service: Whatever little we can offer, God will transform into great blessing. Our need to ask, and to offer. What we need for growing, God always provides.
Mood: Being honest with God and trusting. Reassurance – little by little is fine.

Possibilities for worship:

- Invite everyone to bring a sign of themselves – something to represent their work or character or hobby – and have a big procession at the Offertory, bringing these 'gifts' to offer ourselves along with the bread and wine.

- Have bread being mixed and kneaded at the beginning of the service and the bowl of dough put to rise. If the bread rolls are small they can be baked as well so they are ready to share around afterwards.

- Tell the Gospel (Year B) rather than reading it (almost learn it by heart) and have five loaves and two tins of sardines placed around the church to be found and offered. The Gospel then merges into the talk.

- For Year A have the different examples acted out, and for Year C have the central section acted out.

- Pray the Lord's Prayer using your fingers (see page 114).

Areas of prayer focus around the church:

- Encourage people to pray with their hands open and cupped to receive.

- Have a prayer board with small coloured shapes of paper for prayers to be drawn or written. Explain that God can read it however it's spelt.

- Have the word TRUST written downwards and invite people to add in their prayer sentences beginning wth the appropriate letter (for example: Thank you for . . . Refresh those on holiday . . . Uphold those going through a difficult time . . . Set our hearts on your kingdom . . . Train us to think lovingly . . .).

Sundays after Trinity: Proper 13, Years ABC

(Sunday between 31 July and 6 August)

Year A: Feeding of 5000
Year B: Food of eternal life
Year C: Store up heavenly wealth

Focus of the service: The way God provides for our earthly and spiritual needs.
Mood: Challenging materialism and worldly attitudes. Knowing our need and reliance on God. Receptive to God's gifts. Seeking God's kingdom.

Possibilities for worship:

- In flower arrangements include wheat and flour and bread.
- Projected images of wheat and harvesting, bread and money during the time of confession and forgiveness. Use phrases from the readings with silence linked with 'Lord, have mercy' instead of a formal prayer of confession.
- The Gospel for Years A and C can be dramatised either with mime, spoken parts or human tableaux, with people forming themselves into a couple of set positions as if they are in a painting.
- For Year A, have bread being mixed and kneaded at the beginning of the service and the bowl of dough put to rise. If the bread rolls are small they can be baked as well so they are ready to share around afterwards.
- For Year C, make a special time of the giving, perhaps for a particular local charity, with more collectors than usual, linking the prayers with this and collecting the gifts in baskets.

Areas of prayer focus around the church:

- Have an exhibition of the local charity you are collecting for, so that part of the offering is people's prayers for the needs.
- Link the prayer areas with the flower arrangements and provide candles for lighting as people pray.
- Use the projected images again to help people pray about the needs of our world, both physically and spiritually.

Sundays after Trinity: Proper 14, Years ABC

(Sunday between 7 and 13 August)

Year A: Jesus rescues us wherever we are
Year B: The living bread from heaven
Year C: Be ready to receive the kingdom

Focus of the service: Jesus is always there for us. Are we ready to welcome him?
Mood: Trusting. Thankful. Expectant.

Possibilities for worship:

- Silver, green and blue streamers and flags for Year A. As well as for waving in the singing, they can act out the sea during the Gospel telling. (Even a stormy sea doesn't stop Jesus reaching us.) Green and yellow for Year B, and gold, silver and red for Year C.

- Tell the Gospel in Year A, involving the children in a pretend boat. Have sound effects of the sea. Use different voices for Year B, involving the whole congregation for verse 42, a different voice for the narrator, and the prophecy read out from a 'scroll'. For Year C tell, rather than read, as far as possible, and have children around holding candle lanterns.

- Draw out particular phrases from the readings in bubble writing on a large roll of paper and have paint in sponges for young children to be colouring them, together with old shirt-overalls and a bowl of water.

- Have the candle lanterns also around the altar during the Eucharistic prayer.

Areas of prayer focus around the church:

- Sea-coloured fabric for Year A, with words from the Gospel, 'Take heart, it is I. Do not be afraid!' Green and yellow for Year B, with 'I am the bread of life. Whoever comes to me will never be hungry . . .' Gold, silver and red for Year C, with 'For where your treasure is, there your heart will be as well.' And 'Don't be afraid, little flock, for it is the Father's pleasure to give you the kingdom.'

- Images and headlines of prayer concerns in the local community, the Church and the world, with sticky notes and pens for writing prayers and prayer concerns.

Sundays after Trinity: Proper 15, Years ABC

(Sunday between 14 and 20 August)

Year A: In mercy God rescues us all
Year B: Jesus is our eternal life-bread
Year C: Read the signs

Focus of the service: Cosmic, worldwide healing and feeding.
Mood: Mind-stretching. Thankful. Disturbing.

Possibilities for worship:

- Year A: have the Gospel read as a conversation with different voices acting it out. Year B: have the congregation reading verse 52 of the Gospel, so that the rest is a reply to their question. Year C: have all the different examples of faith, in Hebrews 11, read by a variety of voices.

- Project images of skyscapes with lots of weather threatened, or heavy clouds with the rays of the sun streaming down through them, or a rainbow, the sign of God's promise.

- Under the altar table have a flower arrangement which includes broken bread and wheat, grapes and poured out wine.

- Invite everyone to pray the Lord's Prayer in their own language, or a language they know well.

Areas of prayer focus around the church:

- Place flags together of different countries in conflict at the moment as people pray for the peace of the world.

- Have a world map, with stickers available so people can place it on the area they are praying for.

- Print out particular verses from the readings today for people to colour or decorate as they pray.

Sundays after Trinity: Proper 16, Years ABC

(Sunday between 21 and 27 August)

Year A: 'You are the Son of the living God'
Year B: 'You have words of eternal life'
Year C: Lord of the Sabbath

Focus of the service: Jesus' authority. Who is this Jesus? Jesus is the Son of God.
Mood: Facing up to implications of who Jesus is. Commitment. Awe and wonder. Mystery.

Possibilities for worship:

- Projected and/or displayed images of mystery and majesty in creation: cosmic and dramatic scenery, close-up of detail in butterfly or a drop of water captured just as it splashes.

- Have an image of Christ which is gradually uncovered during the service, so that Christ is fully revealed from being hidden.

- Have someone painting an image of Christ on a large sheet during the service, as their worship.

- Mark out on the floor a maze which little children can lead an adult along into the centre, where there is a picture of Jesus as the Good Shepherd, and the words 'You are the Messiah, the Son of God!'

- In Year A hold hands all over the church during the second reading. In Year B have someone dressed up in the 'armour' during the second reading. In Year C act out the Gospel.

- Give people small arrow-shaped cards with a question mark on one side of them and an exclamation mark on the other. Invite people to use these to focus their own thinking and worship during the service and during the coming week.

- In a creative area provide key phrases from the Gospel for people to write out or decorate in coloured pens as carefully as they can, and take home with them.

Areas of prayer focus around the church:

- Provide one of this week's long-term truths as a striking focus, and surround it with short-term, quick-fix headlines and advertisements roughly cut out.

- Have the words 'Who do YOU say that I am?' in a thought bubble.

- Have a map of the local area and invite people to place candles on the places they are praying for.
- Prayer suggestions: 'Thank God for those who have brought you to faith'; 'Pray for those who are sad'; 'Pray for God's will to be done'.

Sundays after Trinity: Proper 17, Years ABC

(Sunday between 28 August and 3 September)

Year A: Take up your cross and follow me
Year B: Honour God with lips and lives
Year C: Be humble and generous-hearted

Focus of the service: Living godly lives. Overcoming evil with good. The cost of discipleship in humility and obedience.
Mood: Honest, humble and self-aware. Listening and attentive. Sense of the responsibility of our calling.

Possibilities for worship:

- Catch the mood in the music playing as people come in, and the look of the church: try tender, gentle music, either recorded or live from group of instrumentalists, clear the church of clutter and have it really clean and beautiful, with little flower arrangements everywhere, and perhaps a bowl of fragrant incense or oil burning.

- For Year A give everyone a small piece of paper and a pencil as they come in. At the time of confession invite people to draw a capital 'I' as they recall the ways we live selfishly, and then cross it out, forming a cross shape, proclaiming God's forgiving love and our invitation to take up our cross and follow him.

- For Year B give everyone a heart shape to focus on as the Gospel is read (you may wish to lead people into the confession time after the Gospel and talk today).

- For Year C tell the Gospel and involve the children to help you tell it by acting it out. This helps both them and the rest of the congregation to understand the truth of the story.

- Have music as a background to the second reading in all three years, giving people reflective space as the words of advice sink in.

Areas of prayer focus around the church:

- Make a focus with draped fabric, flowers and a cross standing on a mirror, with the words 'May our lives reflect your love.'

- Place images of needs and prayer concerns around the cross with the words.

- Have a cross, or icon, standing on the floor, with hassocks around so that people can kneel and pray – not a fashionable posture in churches at the moment but a valuable one in allowing our bodies to express our reverence.

- Place images of needs and prayer concern around the cross with the words 'Lord, in your mercy, hear our prayer.'

Sundays after Trinity: Proper 18, Years ABC
(Sunday between 4 and 10 September)

Year A: Dealing with conflict and sin
Year B: Healing as a sign of the Son of God
Year C: The cost of discipleship

Focus of the service: Year A: Encouraging one another in godly living. Year B: Jesus heals as the prophets foretold. Year C: Putting God first.
Mood: Year A: Student-mode, learning at the feet of Jesus. Year B: Looking and learning from the signs. Openness. Year C: Cost counting, recognising practicalities.

Possibilities for worship:

- Years A and C: use words from the Old Testament readings (track 2) in the time of confession; Year B: use words from Psalm 146:7-8

- All three years are alerting us to listen and learn. Have a hazard triangle included in an arrangement of red flowers, and while music plays, invite people to look around the church for signs that tell them about God's love.

- Have instruments, bells and streamers of contrasting colours to wave as part of the praise and worship – celebrating the practical signs of God's love.

- At the Peace, pass along a string or wool thread for everyone to hold on to, which winds around the whole congregation and people, demonstrating their close family bond.

- Have a collection of clothing or food and toiletries for a local area of need.

Areas of prayer focus around the church:

- Highlight a local, national or international charity with information and prayer needs shown visually, and invite people to light candles, or build a prayer cairn with stones they pick up and place on one of the focus areas.

- Among headlines and pictures from newspapers of current prayer needs, place cards with prayer suggestions: 'Open our eyes and our ears'; 'Pray for families and churches torn apart by conflict'; 'Comfort those who are hurting and heal their pain'; 'Pray for all who lead others'; 'Pray for God's people to walk humbly with God'.

Sundays after Trinity: Proper 19, Years ABC

(Sunday between 11 and 17 September)

Year A: Forgive as you are forgiven
Year B: Jesus must suffer and die to save us
Year C: Joy in heaven over one repentant sinner

Focus of the service: Our call to reflect God's love, mercy and forgiveness.
Mood: Both challenging and liberating.

Possibilities for worship:

- Year A: try using the Old Testament reading (track 2) as an introduction to the time of confession, so that Joseph's compassion and forgiveness inspires us to put right with God any resentment and bitterness coming from our failure to forgive. Year B: use the words from the Gospel: 'If any want to be my followers, let them deny themselves and take up their cross and follow me.' Year C: use the words from 1 Timothy: 'Christ Jesus came into the world to save sinners.' As God's forgiveness is proclaimed, project an image of the wide sea, have the sounds of the ocean, and sing something like 'I'm accepted, I'm forgiven'.

- Be lavish and generous with praise and worship, full of thankfulness for God's saving love. Wave banners, streamers or flags, and give out bells and percussion instruments.

- Wrap wire netting around a rough wooden cross and decorate it with flowers during the Gloria and the readings.

- Act out the parable in Year A's Gospel. Have the Isaiah reading from Year B spoken with a group of voices, chorally. Involve the children in the telling of the lost sheep and lost coin parables in Year C.

- Play the *Miserere* by Allegri (the psalm for Year C) during Communion.

Areas of prayer focus around the church:

- Give everyone a penny to focus on as they are led to pray for those who are very poor, those in debt, those in prisons of different kinds, for the round world and its resources, for the Queen and for all world leaders.

- Cut out footprints and fix them to the floor leading people to the font or to a cross or particular window, where the words 'Take up your cross and follow me' are written.

- Provide pictures and prayer suggestions placed on green fabric, with a bowl of water and a candle floating in it. Invite people to place small flower heads on the water as they pray for people's needs.

Sundays after Trinity: Proper 20, Years ABC

(Sunday between 18 and 24 September)

Year A: God longs to save every person
Year B: Being greatest means being a servant
Year C: You can't serve God and wealth

Focus of the service: God's values are different from worldly ones.
Mood: Thankfulness for God's generous heart of love. Challenging.
Inspiring.

Possibilities for worship:

- Have phrases from the readings written out for colouring in and decorating. (Or give out letters and together build them into the whole phrase.) Year A: 'I choose to give to this last one the same as I give to you . . . Are you envious because I am generous?' Year B: 'Whoever wants to be first must be last of all and servant of all.' Year C: 'You cannot serve God and wealth.'

- Year A: act out the Gospel or have different voices speaking it. Year B: act out the Gospel. 'Through Galilee' is through the body of the church, with 'Capernaum' the front of the church. Make sure that 'Jesus' is someone the little child knows well and trusts. Year C: act the parable in the Gospel – it's quite a pantomime style story.

- Images projected of the world, or crowds of people, during the last part of Year A's Gospel (verses 13-160), Year B's gospel (verses 33-37) and Year C's Gospel (verses 10-13).

- Bring out the message of each Gospel in one of the flower arrangements. Incorporate scales with the two bowls holding an equivalent weight – one labelled 'the first' and the other 'the last' (Year A), apron, towel and water (Year B), and bags of monopoly money (Year C).

Areas of prayer focus around the church:

- Suggestions for prayer: 'Pray for those who have wronged you and make life a misery for you'; 'Pray for a more generous outlook'; 'Pray for all those who have come in and out of the church door'; 'Pray for those whose insecurity makes them vulnerable'.

- Have green fabric draped near the font filled with water. Float a candle in the font. Pray for the world, the Church, your own loved ones, for all who suffer and for those who have died. Drop a small pebble in the font as you pray for people.

- Have pictures of those leaders in the headlines this week, and also those who are unknown and voiceless.

Sundays after Trinity: Proper 21, Years ABC

(Sunday between 25 September and 1 October)

Year A: Life – God's choice. Our choice?
Year B: Don't risk losing eternal life
Year C: Wealth can make us blind

Focus of the service: God longs for us to have abundant life and complete fulfilment. Learning how to make good life choices through God's live-in help.
Mood: Challenging and inspiring. Serious and important learning.

Possibilities for worship:

- Year A: involve a group of voices to speak the words of the chief priests and elders in the gospel. Year B: have different voices speaking the parts in the Old Testament story of Moses and God's Spirit. Year C: involve the whole congregation as the Israelites, and separate voices for Moses and for God in the Old Testament reading (track 2).

- Use music with an 'ache' in it to accompany the second reading in Year A (starting at verse 3), the Gospel in Year B (starting at verse 41) and the Old Testament reading (track 2) in Year C.

- Project an image of sunlit autumn leaves to accompany the psalm in all three years. It makes a point of mortality without any words being spoken.

- Year A: use verses 5-11 of Philippians 4 as a credal statement.

- Year B: include sea salt, sea lavender, shells and pebbles in a flower arrangement, and beside it write out Mark 9:50

- Year C: make a display near the door as people come in which includes uprooted weeds and symbols of affluence like money and cards, 'growing' into dead thorny branches together with some dried and garishly coloured plants, next to an arrangement of tiny fresh foliage and white flowers. Write out as a title 1 Timothy 10.

Areas of prayer focus around the church:

- For Year B use the salty flower arrangement as a prayer focus, with a bowl of salt so people can dip their fingers in it as they pray, 'Keep us salty for the good of the world'.

- Have a collection for money and/or food and clothes, at a prayer area which focuses on the needs of the homeless or hungry. Use pictures and information to help people pray, so that the giving and praying go hand in hand.

- Make a prayer wall with a length of lining paper and have a few prayers and drawings already on it. Leave plenty of pens and crayons beside it so people can write or draw their prayers.

Sundays after Trinity: Proper 22, Years ABC

(Sunday between 2 and 8 October)

Year A: The vineyard and its tenants
Year B: Even little children are welcomed
Year C: Being obedient servants of God

Focus of the service: Freedom in God's service. Our privileges and responsibilities as the people of God.
Mood: Thought-provoking and challenging expectations. Love and harmony of fulfilment as we meet in God's presence. Awe and reverence.

Possibilities for worship:

- Have a sense of ongoing worship as people walk into the church, rather than waiting for 'the service' to start.
- Have several places around the church where there is a beautiful window, or a picture, or prayer focus, each with one candle alight, and as people come in give them a candle. Invite them to choose where they light and place their candle. As the church fills with people, so it fills with lights.
- At the offertory, have children bringing small bowls of burning incense or potpourri and placing them on the floor around the altar table.
- Project pictures of grapes (Year A), of people – men, women and children – (Year B), and of foot-washing (Year C).
- Use music to help create a climate of worship and reverence in the living presence of God. Try something slightly different from what people are used to hearing – from another culture, or the Hilliard Ensemble with the jazz saxophonist Jan Garbarek.
- Years A and C: the Isaiah 5:1-7 and the Habakkuk readings can be done effectively as a rap. Year B: Accompany the Genesis reading with projected images of creation.

Areas of prayer focus around the church:

- Invite people to walk around the church, praying as they go, and stopping at the different prayer focuses now lit with candles. Have one focused on the world, with a globe, one on the Church, with a church made of children's building blocks, one on our community, with pictures of people, and one of those who are suffering, with a first aid box and a tear, cut from shiny wrapping paper or foil. Or invite people to stand at any one of the prayer areas and pray together in small groups of twos or threes.

Sundays after Trinity: Proper 23, Years ABC

(Sunday between 9 and 15 October)

Year A: Wedding invitations and excuses
Year B: Wealth can get in the way of the kingdom
Year C: The ten lepers are healed

Focus of the service: God's generous invitation. Our response.
Mood: Gracious generosity and sense of God's welcome and acceptance.

Possibilities for worship:

- Include an opportunity for first-time or deeper commitment in response to God's invitation. Make this a healing service – see suggestions for prayer below.
- Involve plenty of people in the acting out of the Gospel parable in Year A, with people collected from the pews (or even outside the church if they'll come!) to join in the wedding feast.
- Act out the meeting and conversation with the young man who was wealthy in the Gospel for Year B, using the whole church.
- Act out the Gospel in Year C. The welcoming back of the lepers into the community is a powerful visual symbol of what Jesus' proclaiming of the kingdom was all about.
- Worship flags to wave and dance with. Fragrant oil burner.
- Decorate the church a bit to reflect the setting of today's teaching – the wedding feast in Year A, the pull of wealth away from the kingdom in Year B (make a collage of advertisements and financial advice; give everyone a coin as they come in), and in Year C the lepers bandaged and ringing their bells, hanging around the church entrance as people arrive.

Areas of prayer focus around the church:

- If this is a healing service give space during the prayers for people to pray with one another (all ages), to have hands laid on them, to be anointed with oil or washed at the font.
- Encourage everyone to pray during this time, providing quiet music and hymns of worship, with opportunity to light candles and write or draw prayers.

Sundays after Trinity: Proper 24, Years ABC
(Sunday between 16 and 22 October)

Year A: Give to God what is God's
Year B: Jesus came not to be served but to serve
Year C: God hears our cries and helps us

Focus of the service: Our relationship with Jesus. Knowing God helps us know ourselves.
Mood: Comforting and inspiring through God's acceptance of us.

Possibilities for worship:

- As they come in give people a text verse for today: 'I call you by your name' (Year A), 'By his bruises we are healed' (Year B), and 'The Lord himself watches over you' (Year C).

- During the time of confession and forgiveness, invite people to hold on to their text and let God's forgiving love heal and set them free.

- Streamers of different colours to wave and bells to ring during the Gloria and the Sanctus.

- At the collection, have an offering of ourselves as well as our gifts. Invite everyone to walk out of their seats, come up and bow or place their hand on the cross so as to make an offering of themselves, and then return to their seat.

- Have the conversations in the Gospel spoken by different voices in Year A and B. Have the Year C Gospel mimed as it is read.

Areas of prayer focus around the church:

- Select verses from the readings to help people focus their prayers, with headlines and pictures of prayer concerns and the human condition among tiny posy arrangements of flowers, and candles.

- Have mirrors and the words, 'It is the Lord who will keep you safe.'

- Prayer suggestions: 'Offer God your past week and the week ahead'; 'In your imagination, stand alongside those who are living in danger and fear'.

Sundays after Trinity: Proper 25, Years ABC

(Sunday between 23 and 29 October)

Year A: Love God, love your neighbour
Year B: Opening the eyes of God's people
Year C: 'God be merciful to me, a sinner'

Focus of the service: God's holiness heals our blindness and makes us holy.

Mood: Open to receive God's gifts of healing and forgiveness. Responsive to God's love for us.

Possibilities for worship:

- Encourage people to receive God's gifts of healing and forgiveness throughout the worship, and particularly as they come to receive the bread and wine or a blessing. Give out candles to those who receive a blessing, so they can go and light them as they thank God for all his blessings to them.

- The worship group Wellspring have recorded a blessing which they have prayed and played over people. Use this, or a home-grown instrumental group playing as everyone is sharing in the bread and wine.

- Year A: have the words from Leviticus 19:18 written large for ongoing communal decorating through the worship.

- Year B: have the conversation between Jesus and BarTimaeus acted out in the gospel, with BarTimaeus far away from Jesus when he starts shouting. Perhaps the churchwardens can go and fetch him to Jesus.

- Year C: in the Gospel reading have the Pharisee stationed in the middle of the congregation, shouting out his prayer from there, and the tax-collector from the back of the church, whispering into a microphone.

- Project pictures of God's glory in creation with the words, 'Lord, have mercy' printed on another, overlaid acetate. Use this as a focus for the time of confession and forgiveness, rather than using words.

Areas of prayer focus around the church:

- As music is playing, and people are moving about praying, project some images of the local area with its needs, together with the words, 'Lord, have mercy'.

- Use green fabric to drape and place a few pictures of people caring for our world and for one another. Place candles on a mirror and the words, 'You shall be holy, for I the Lord your God am holy' (Year A), 'The Lord has done great things for us and we are glad indeed' (Year B), and 'Happy are those whose strength is in you' (Year C).
- Prayer suggestions: 'Pray for the grace to forgive any who have hurt you'; 'Ask God to show you any prejudices you are unaware of, and to heal you of them'; 'Pray for those you strongly disagree with'.

Sundays after Trinity: Bible Sunday, Years ABC

(Sunday between 23 and 29 October)

Year A: My words will never pass away
Year B: Moses wrote about me
Year C: Today this scripture is fulfilled

Focus of the service: Thanksgiving for the holy scriptures and their witness to Jesus.
Mood: Thankful reverence for the word of God.

Possibilities for worship:

- Have a display of Bible reading notes and guides for all ages, and encourage the daily habit.
- Display a whole range of Bible editions, old and new, together with a model of biblical scrolls and maps of the Holy Land, around a loaf of bread in a basket on a white cloth, and a candle or candle lantern.
- Read one of the readings all together, printing it out for different voices – men and boys, women and girls, and single voices, or right and left sides of the church.
- Invite people to share particular verses which have been life-changing.
- Use the words from Philippians 2:6-11 or 1 Corinthians 15:3-7 as a credal statement.

Areas of prayer focus around the church:

- Make the Bible display one of the prayer areas.
- Have a Bible open at today's Gospel in the centre of each prayer focus with a candle burning, and the words, 'Your word is a lamp to my feet'.
- Take the intentions for prayer from the Bible and print them on separate cards, placed among pictures of the good creation and those in need.
- Prayer suggestions: 'Watch and pray so that you will not fall into temptation'; 'Pray to the Lord for one another'; 'Pray for those who persecute you'; 'Pray for the peace of Jerusalem'; 'Pray for unity'; 'Pray that you may be active in sharing'.

Dedication Sunday, Years ABC
(First Sunday in October or Last Sunday after Trinity)

Year A: A house of prayer
Year B: You are living stones
Year C: The temple of Jesus' body

Focus of the service: Rededication of the church as building and as people for God's service.
Mood: Celebration and thanksgiving.

Possibilities for worship:

- Banners made by different groups within the church.
- Brightly coloured streamers and flags to wave in worship during the singing.
- Bells and instruments to accompany some of the hymns and Gloria.
- A thorough clean-up of the church and de-cluttering done as worship on the Saturday before today by people of all ages.
- A shared lunch together after worship, with an exhibition of pictures from the past years at the church, or a church video shot during the year.
- Representatives of all age groups in the readings, collection, singing and playing and refreshments.
- Have on display the Baptismal and Wedding Registers, and any other symbols of the church's character and history.
- Encourage people to form prayer triplets for committed shared prayer times during the coming year. All ages can be included in this.

Areas of prayer focus around the church:

- Highlight all the special places in your building and place an appropriate Bible verse by each.
- Invite people either to move around the building, using these places for prayers of thanksgiving and intercession, or to pray in small groups in their seats, depending on size of congregation.
- Prayer suggestions: 'Pray for all who walk in and out of this place'; 'Pray for those who have been married here'; 'Pray for those who have been baptised in this font'; 'Thank God for all who have worshipped here through their lives'; 'Pray that this community may be a true sign of God's kingdom'.

All Saints' Sunday, Years ABC

(Sunday between 30 October and 5 November, if kept on the Sunday)

Focus of the service: A celebration of those whose lives reflect God's love and inspire us.
Mood: Joyful and thankful.

Possibilities for worship:

- Children (and adults if they want!) can come dressed up as different saints.
- Everyone holds a lighted candle at the Gospel and during the Eucharistic Prayer and Lord's Prayer.
- Instruments, streamers and flags for worship during the singing.
- A praise wall of lining paper, with crayons available, with a few prayers and drawings already on it to give an example, together with a written invitation to add your own.
- Projected image of sun streaming through clouds during the Collect and readings.
- Music of mystery and wonder played as a background to a communal reading of the first reading.
- Sweets given out for people to suck during the short talk to 'taste the sweetness of God's love'.

Areas of prayer focus around the church:

- Use any stained glass windows, praying for God's love to shine through your life so that people see it and glorify God.
- Have tissue paper stained glass pictures mounted on plain glass or projected using the OHP.
- At the font, pray for those recently baptised or confirmed, and for those who are struggling with doubts, or persecution for their faith. Have the font full of water, with candles floating on it.

Fourth Sunday before Advent, Years ABC

(Sunday between 30 October and 5 November)

Year A: Jesus speaks of the end of the age
Year B: Love God and love your neighbour
Year C: Jesus came to save the lost

Focus of the service: Putting things right with God.
Mood: Shifting towards preparation for Advent. Getting back to the basics of our faith.

Possibilities for worship:

- Red streamers and flags for worship.
- Pumpkin lanterns around the church, with cross-shaped holes cut out of them.
- Year A: have music with a sense of the disturbing as a background to the Gospel reading. Year B: have the Gospel read by different voices as a conversation. Year C: involve the children in acting out the Gospel reading.
- Use the Summary of the Law as part of the time of confession and words of God's forgiveness, while an image of storm clouds with a rainbow is projected.

Areas of prayer focus around the church:

- Use red fabric draped, and images of worldwide human needs placed among prayer suggestions.
- Have a globe standing on a shiny surface with candles around it.
- Encourage people to pray for God's guidance in one another's lives, not just now but throughout the week.
- Prayer suggestions: 'Pray for the grace to listen to one another this week'; 'Pray for the courage to stand up for goodness, justice and mercy'; 'Pray for God to transform any difficult relationships'; 'Pray for God to be in your thinking and your choices'.

Third Sunday before Advent, Years ABC

(Sunday between 6 and 12 November)

Year A: Keeping ourselves ready
Year B: The kingdom of God has come near: follow me
Year C: Life beyond death

Focus of the service: Life with a heavenly dimension.
Mood: Exciting and with a sense of adventuring.

Possibilities for worship:

- Red is the colour – around the church and in the streamers.
- The pumpkin lanterns again, with cross-shaped light holes.
- Just before the Gloria, light the Easter candle and invite everyone to sit perfectly and completely still, sharing stillness in the presence of the great Holy Spirit of God. Let the praise of the Gloria pour out of this awareness of the heavenly in the earthly.
- Have the children holding candles around the altar table at the Eucharistic Prayer.
- Write out a verse from the readings for the day in bubble writing to be coloured in or decorated.
- Have a display of a backpack and map and compass, and a small cross on a string or chain, with the words 'Follow me' beside it.

Areas of prayer focus around the church:

- Red fabric, and pictures of sunrise and wide landscape beckoning you into the distance.
- Use the backpack display as one prayer focus, inviting people to pray for a renewed sense of adventure on their own faith journey with Jesus, and for those who are encouraging us along the way.
- Provide candles for people to light as they remember their loved ones who have died. Nearby have the words from 1 Thessalonians 4:14-18.
- Prayer suggestions: 'Commit your week to God's guiding and be prepared for anything'; 'Ask God to show you opportunities for generous loving'; 'Pray for God to bring healing and freedom to locked-up lives'.

Second Sunday before Advent, Years ABC

(Sunday between 13 and 19 November)

Year A: Be ready by making use of God's gifts
Year B: Don't fear the disturbing future
Year C: Fear not – I'll be with you

> **Focus of the service:** God's reassuring presence will help us cope with the frightening end-times.
> **Mood:** Bracing ourselves for a disturbing future, but confident in Jesus' love and protection.

Possibilities for worship:

- Red streamers and banners or flags.
- Red and orange crayons and self-adhesive labels to decorate the verse of the week: Year A: 'Well done, good and faithful servant!'; Year B: 'In your presence there is fullness of joy'; Year C: 'By standing firm you will gain life'.
- Year A: act out the Gospel, either miming it as it is narrated, or dramatising it with different speaking parts. Years B and C: during the Gospel project an image of ancient ruins, and bring in some film music from verse 3/verse 6 onwards which picks up on the atmosphere of disturbing times ahead.
- During the service have someone invited to be painting on a large hanging sheet, to express the peace of God leading us through all danger to eternal life.
- Invite everyone to receive £1 and make it grow by using it well over the coming month. The proceeds can then be presented to a charity for Christmas, with love from the church. Commission people for this adventure as part of the service today.

Areas of prayer focus around the church:

- The colour is red again this week.
- Have a candle surrounded with barbed wire (take great care) and pray for all those who are imprisoned, whether by bars or poverty, guilt or fear.
- Have a small pot of incense or fragrant oil burning to express the prayers rising to heaven.
- Have a prayer book of pictures and headlines which can be added to by people as they pray.

Christ the King, Years ABC
(Sunday between 20 and 26 November)

Year A: As you did to them, you did to me
Year B: 'My kingdom is not of this world'
Year C: The image of the unseen God

Focus of the service: Jesus Christ the King.
Mood: Mysterious, reverent, challenging, celebrational.

Possibilities for worship:

- Red and gold streamers and banners for waving and dancing with during some of the singing.
- A trumpet (or recorders) to herald the start of the worship with a fanfare.
- Paper crowns to decorate, make and wear, as sons and daughters of the King.
- Projected images of Christ as the Good Shepherd, foot washing, and as the Light of the World. Use these during the readings and the Eucharistic Prayer.
- Large printed verses from the day's readings to colour or decorate so the verses can be displayed. For instance, Year A: 'I myself will be the shepherd of my sheep'; Year B: 'My kingdom is not of this world'; Year C: 'Jesus, remember me when you come into your kingdom'.
- Invite people to be anointed with oil marked in a cross on their forehead as a sign of welcoming Jesus' reign in their whole life.

Areas of prayer focus around the church:

- Red and gold cloth with a gold crown placed on it, surrounded by candles and small arrangements of red and gold flowers in lids.
- Write out prayer suggestions and place them among pictures, names and situations needing our prayers.
- Have a globe, or a world map, and sticky notes so people can write or draw their prayers and stick them on the part of the world they apply to.
- Prayer suggestions: 'Pray for God's kingdom to come and God's will to be done'; 'Pray for all who make important decisions in the world'; 'Pray for the downtrodden and oppressed'; 'Pray for evil plans to be thwarted and good plans to be blessed'; 'Pray that we may act justly, love with mercy and walk humbly with God'.

Harvest Festival

Harvest Festival doesn't have a set time in the Church year, so the time to celebrate it can be arranged to suit local needs. It happens at some point during September or October, and remains one of the best-loved and widely remembered occasions for many people, so is a marvellous opportunity for outreach. It is important to make Harvest services as accessible as possible, involving the local community and addressing its particular needs.

Possibilities for worship:
- Yellow, red and green drapes of light, cheap fabric to display the gifts provided.
- Create an impression of the good earth producing these gifts, with perhaps a globe, flowers and vegetables in striking and unusual arrangements, a mirror with earth and pebbles and small plants around it, a sheaf of wheat and so on.
- Or try a seascape impression, with nets and oars, a mirror and sand and shells around its edge; or a rain forest with a loaned collection of houseplants, bright coloured wooden parrots on sticks, and bright flowering plants edging the mirror.
- Check with local agencies and night shelters so that you can ask people to bring a selection of the items needed, and take them along with a card assuring them of your prayers.
- Either have the food decorating the church in place before the service, or make this a festive procession of thanksgiving at the collection and offertory.
- Have brightly coloured streamers and instruments to accompany the music.

Areas of prayer focus around the church:
- Use the beautifully decorated church as a focus for prayer, either inviting people to wander around it looking and praying as uplifting music is quietly played (either recorded or live) or, if the church is full, suggest that while the music plays people sit and look around them, rejoicing in God's gifts as they pray.
- Prayer suggestions: 'Pray for those who provide our food'; 'Pray for those who go hungry'; 'Pray for the commitment to share the world's resources fairly'; 'Pray for the grace to live more simply so that others may simply live'.

Resources

The daily readings

Day 1 – Genesis 1:1 In the beginning God created the heavens and the earth.

Day 2 – Genesis 1:31 God saw everything that he had made and indeed it was very good.

Day 3 – Psalm 18:28 It is you who lights my lamp; the Lord my God lights up my darkness.

Day 4 – Psalm 51:10 Create in me a clean heart, O God, and put a new and right spirit within me.

Day 5 – Psalm 55:16 I call upon God and the Lord will save me.

Day 6 – Isaiah 25:9 This is the Lord for whom we have waited. Let us be glad and rejoice that he saves us.

Day 7 – Isaiah 33:22 The Lord is our King; he will save us.

Day 8 – Isaiah 35:4 Say to those who are of a fearful heart, 'Be strong, do not fear! Here is your God.'

Day 9 – Isaiah 43:1 Do not fear, for I have redeemed you. I have called you by name, you are mine.

Day 10 – Isaiah 60:1 Arise, shine; for your light has come and the glory of the Lord has risen upon you.

Day 11 – John 1:9 The true light, which lights up everyone, was coming into the world.

Day 12 – Luke 1:30 Do not be afraid, Mary, for you have found favour with God.

Day 13 – Luke 1:31 You will bear a son and you will call him Jesus.

Day 14 – Luke 1:32 He will be great and will be called the Son of the Most High.

Day 15 – Luke 1:46-47 And Mary said . . . 'My spirit rejoices in God my Saviour.'

Day 16 – Matthew 1:20 Joseph, son of David, do not be afraid to take Mary as your wife.

Day 17 – Matthew 1:21 She will bear a son and you are to name him Jesus for he will save his people from their sins.

Day 18 – Luke 2:4 Joseph went to be registered at Bethlehem with Mary who was expecting a baby.

Day 19 – Luke 2:7 While they were there she gave birth to her firstborn son.

Day 20 – Luke 2:7 She wrapped the baby in bands of cloth and laid him in a manger because there was no room in the inn.

Day 21 – Luke 2:8 There were shepherds living in the fields, keeping watch over their flocks by night.

Day 22 – Luke 2:9 An angel of the Lord appeared, and the glory of the Lord shone around them, and they were terrified.

Day 23 – Luke 2:11 The angel said, 'To you is born this day in the city of David a Saviour, who is the Messiah, the Lord.'

Day 24 – Luke 2:16 So they hurried off and found Mary and Joseph and the child lying in the manger.

Day 25 – John 1:14 The Word became flesh and lived among us, and we have seen his glory.

Gloria shout

Who was there before anything else? GOD WAS!
Who decided to make this world? GOD DID!
Who is in charge of the world for ever? GOD IS!

Who was walking on earth as Jesus? GOD WAS!
Who loves us so much that he died for us all? GOD DID!
Who is alive in us now through his Spirit? GOD IS!

Who do we believe in? WE BELIEVE IN GOD!

The Lord's Prayer on your fingers

As you pray, hold each finger in turn.

Hold your thumb, reminding you that you are human, as you pray to God as your heavenly Father:

OUR FATHER WHO ART IN HEAVEN, HALLOWED BE THY NAME.

Hold your index finger, the finger of authority, as you pray for God to be in charge:

THY KINGDOM COME. THY WILL BE DONE ON EARTH AS IT IS IN HEAVEN.

Hold your middle finger to open out your hand into a receiving position as you pray:

GIVE US THIS DAY OUR DAILY BREAD.

Hold your ring finger, reminding you of relationships with other people as you pray:

AND FORGIVE US OUR TRESPASSES AS WE FORGIVE THOSE WHO TRESPASS AGAINST US.

Hold your weak little finger, remembering how much you need God's strength, as you pray:

LEAD US NOT INTO TEMPTATION BUT DELIVER US FROM EVIL.

Either put both hands together, or raise them as you pray:

FOR THINE IS THE KINGDOM, THE POWER AND THE GLORY, FOR EVER AND EVER. AMEN.

Men and boys:

We thank you for the friendship we have shared tonight and for the loving kindness you shower on us each day.

All:

We thank you for freeing us from slavery and sin through the gift of your forgiveness.
We pray that all God's children may be freed from hatred and hunger, oppression and guilt, free to live contentedly in your love. Amen.

Everyone drinks their wine or grape juice

Leader:

Let us go in God's peace.
Peace for us and peace for all people in the world.
No more war. No more oppression.
Justice and peace for everyone.
Let it be so. **Amen. Let it be so.**

Everyone sings 'Shalom, my friends'

A Passover Celebration

Order of service

1. The candle lighting

The leader welcomes everyone to the Passover, which is a celebration of the way God rescues his people from slavery. Everyone is asked to keep silence as they get ready to receive God's blessing at this Passover meal.

A short time of silence

The leader lights the candles, saying:

Blessed are you, Lord God of all creation.
Of your goodness we have the gift of light
to lighten our darkness.

The light is passed all around the tables until every candle in the room is lit. 'The Lord is my light' (Taizé) may be sung quietly. As this is happening the leader prays:

May the brightness of these small lights
remind us of the great light of your love
which brings us joy and hope.

Blessed be God for ever!

2. We say Grace

We fill our glasses and raise them as we pray:

Blessed are you, Lord God of all creation.
Through your goodness we have this wine to drink,
fruit of the vine and work of human hands.

Blessed be God for ever!

Everyone drinks their wine or grape juice and fills the glass again.

3. We wash our hands

As we wash our fingers in the bowl of water we pray:

7. The meal

The meal is eaten.

8. Hide and seek

After the meal the children can search for the afikomen (the hidden piece of matzo) and the one who finds it is given a reward. This piece of bread is broken and shared out among everyone. The bread is held as the leader says:

This bread is broken and shared to remind us of the Passover lambs which were sacrificed and shared, to give the people strength for their journey ahead and protection from the plague of death.

Everyone eats the fragment of bread.

9. Grace after the meal

Leader:
The Bible tells us that when you have eaten and are satisfied you shall thank the Lord our God for the good land which he has given you. We have eaten and are satisfied, so let us thank God now.

Everyone raises their glasses as they pray:

All:
O Lord our God, we praise you
and thank you for feeding us all in body and spirit.

Women and girls:
We thank you for the good earth
and its fruitfulness.

A song is sung, such as 'Our God is so great, so strong and so mighty', 'You shall go out with joy', 'Give me joy in my heart' or 'Jubilate everybody'.

Blessed are you, Lord God of all creation.
You alone can make us clean.
You alone can make us holy.
Blessed be God for ever!

(At the Last Supper it was not just hands that were washed, but feet as well.)

4. Eating a springtime herb

The leader dips some of the parsley into the salty water, saying:

Blessed are you, Lord God of all creation.
Each springtime, through your goodness,
the earth brings forth plants and fruit,
to renew the world we inhabit.
Blessed be God for ever!

Everyone dips some parsley in salty water and eats it.

5. The bread-sharing

The leader picks up the three pieces of matzo, and puts aside half a piece for unexpected guests, saying:

Blessed are you, Lord God of all creation.
Through your goodness we have this bread to eat
which earth has given and human hands have made.
Let us always share our bread with the hungry.
We remember now all those who are persecuted or poor.
Next year may we and they be free.
Our Passover cannot be complete
until all God's people are free.
Blessed be God for ever!

This is the bread of pain and affliction
which our ancestors ate in Egypt, when they were slaves,
and which our oppressed brothers and sisters eat now.
Take this, all of you, and eat it.

---

that night. This was the tenth and last plague before Pharaoh agreed to let Moses and the people go. Let us express our compassion for the Egyptians who suffered those plagues. They were our enemies, but still they were children of God and fellow human beings, and we feel sorry for all who suffer – whether they are friends or enemies.

As each plague is mentioned, everyone dips a finger in their wine and drips it on their plate to remember the suffering:

Blood . . . Frogs . . . Vermin . . . Flies . . . Cattle disease . . . Boils . . . Hailstones . . . Locusts . . . Darkness . . Death of every firstborn.

Child:

Why are we taking so much trouble over this meal tonight – with clean cloths and candles and flowers and party food?

Because thanks to God's loving rescue, we have all been set free from slavery and sin! In spite of all the tears and sadness in our world there is lots and lots to thank God for, and we want to enjoy thanking him as well as we can for all he has done in our lives.
Blessed be God for ever!

Everyone drinks their wine or grape juice, and refills the glass.

Leader:

Now we are ready to enjoy the Passover meal!

All:

We'll taste the bitterness of pain and oppression
and the sweetness of hope and freedom.
We'll eat thankfully of all God's gifts
and rejoice that we can share this time
and this food together in God's company.

The leader shares the bread with those around, and everyone else shares the bread near them with one another, dipping it in the salty water of tears, remembering the poor and oppressed. The piece of bread put aside is now hidden, for the children to find later on.

Leader:

Let one of the children open our door to show that we welcome all who are hungry, in body and in spirit.

One of the children opens the door wide.

All:

Let all who hunger for bread and for freedom, for truth, and for inner peace, come and share the bread which our God provides for us.

6. The story

The children:

Why is this night different from all other nights?

Leader:

Thank you for asking that question, children. It is always good to ask questions, and find out the answers. That way you will learn the story we share and understand the traditions we value.

Tonight is different from all other nights because we are celebrating something amazing. Once our ancestors were slaves of Pharaoh in Egypt, and God rescued our people, bringing us out of slavery into the promise of freedom and redemption. Our terrible suffering was turned into a time of happiness and blessing.

Child:

Why do we eat only flat bread without yeast tonight?

When Pharaoh let the people go they had to escape in a great hurry. They had no time to wait for their bread to rise, so they baked it flat, like the bread we are eating tonight.

Child:

Why do we eat bitter herbs tonight?

The bitter herbs remind us that life was bitter and sad for the people when they were oppressed as slaves in the land of Egypt. When we taste the bitter herbs we taste the bitterness of every person who is sad and oppressed, and longs to be free.

Child:

Why do we have the sweet stuff to eat?

The sweet stuff reminds us of the sweetness of freedom when God brought us out of slavery. It reminds us of the sweetness of God's goodness and love which always triumphs over evil.

Child:

Why do we eat parsley?

We have parsley because it reminds us of all the fresh green plants of springtime which bring fresh new life to the world each year. Our God loves us and looks after us, and that makes us happy.

Child:

Why do we dip our parsley and bread in salt water?

The salt water reminds us of tears which people cry when they are very sad. As we taste the salty water we remember the tears of the people when they were slaves, and the tears of everyone who is not free or at peace with God.

Child:

Why is there a lamb bone?

Because the people ate a lamb that last night in Egypt, just before they were rescued. They put its blood on their doorposts and so they were protected from the plague of death